T0360612

Sport Branding Insights

In a sporting world dominated by media and money, an understanding of sport branding is an essential skill for any sport manager. Success means being able to 'brand' – and therefore differentiate – a sport club, player, code, or event in a highly competitive entertainment market. For anyone seeking to understand or manage sport, this book offers an immediate and salient insight into the complex and dynamic process of creating a powerful sport brand.

The book explains how a sport brand goes beyond just an identifying badge, reinforced by a name or a logo that helps sport consumers recognise a product or an organisation. It reveals how a brand becomes linked with consumers' opinions and perceptions of a sport product and the organisation that owns it. Readers will learn how to create a powerful brand that has both recognition in the market and strong associated imagery, by imbuing it with a spirit of the past through appeals to tradition, by endowing it with human qualities of emotionality, thought, and volition, and through the use of characters, colours, texts, and symbols. It also provides a brief guide to the new domains of digital sport branding and social media.

Concise, informative, and entertaining, this is an essential resource for anyone exploring or practising the business of sport.

Constantino Stavros is Associate Professor of Marketing at RMIT University, Australia. He is one of Australia's leading media commentators on marketing and branding matters. His research interests lie predominantly at the intersection of consumption and communication.

Aaron C.T. Smith is Professor of Sport Business at the Institute for Sport Business, Loughborough University London. His research investigates psychological, organisational, and policy change in sport, business, health, religion, technology, and society.

Sport Business Insights

Series Editors:
Aaron C.T. Smith, Loughborough University London, UK
Constantino Stavros, RMIT University, Australia

Sport Business Insights is a series that aims to cut through the clutter, providing concise and relevant introductions to an array of contemporary topics related to the business of sport. Readers – including passionate practitioners, curious consumers, and sport students alike - will discover direct and succinct volumes, carefully curated to present a useful blend of practice and theory. In a highly readable format, and prepared by leading experts, this series shines a spotlight on subjects of currency in sport business, offering a systematic guide to critical concepts and their practical application.

Available in this series:

Sport Branding Insights
Constantino Stavros and Aaron C.T. Smith

Sport Branding Insights

**Constantino Stavros
and Aaron C.T. Smith**

Routledge
Taylor & Francis Group

LONDON AND NEW YORK

First published 2020
by Routledge
2 Park Square, Milton Park, Abingdon, Oxon OX14 4RN

and by Routledge
52 Vanderbilt Avenue, New York, NY 10017

Routledge is an imprint of the Taylor & Francis Group, an informa business

British Library Cataloguing-in-Publication Data
A catalogue record for this book is available from the British Library

Library of Congress Cataloging-in-Publication Data
A catalog record has been requested for this book

ISBN: 978-0-367-33164-1 (hbk)
ISBN: 978-0-429-31824-5 (ebk)

Typeset in Times New Roman
by codeMantra

Contents

The sport of branding

Athletes and coaches often refer to the way their team performs as a 'brand' of play. They note that their brand is about entertainment, physical pressure, attacking flair, or similar descriptors. The co-opting of the term brand is purposeful in that the athletes and coaches are seeking to identify something that goes beyond simpler terms like style, tactics, or function. They are attempting to capture an ethos, a belief system, and a conglomeration of thinking that connects them to their fans on a level beyond what is just visible.

This book, however, is not about that sort of branding. While the brand of the team in a playing sense is fundamental to the entertainment that sport provides billions around the world, the recipe for sporting success is being forged not on the whiteboards of coaches, but on those of marketers and sport managers, who understand that in the high-stakes 'game of games,' a long-term brand that remains resilient and respected is a winner year after year.

This book is also not just about the look, slogan, colours, or name of a sporting team, league, product, or entity. While those prosaic elements are often regarded as representations of the brand, and often thought to *be* the brand, as this book will show branding goes beyond symbols and logos. A brand is multifaceted and, surprisingly to many, entirely fluid and enigmatic when it comes to control and ownership. You can trademark a brand element, but a brand's value lies not in the legal paperwork, but in the hearts and minds of the consumers who interact with its learned and shared meanings, both tangible and intangible.

In a sporting world dominated by media and money, an understanding of sport branding constitutes an increasingly essential component in a sport manager's suite of professional capacities. Success means being able to 'brand' – and therefore differentiate – a sport club, player, code, product, or event in a highly competitive entertainment market. Failure means struggling with commercial anonymity and fan disdain. This book aims to provide an immediate and intuitive insight into the complex and dynamic process of creating a powerful sport brand.

All brands begin with a complex set of tangible and intangible associations that exist in the minds of consumers long before they become household icons and shopping centre gridlocks. As such, they are formed through a combination of various elements and the subsequent associations ascribed to these by sport consumers, or, as they are more commonly known, fans. These fans, a term literally derived from the concept of fanaticism, resonate the linkages and associations that can confer a sporting brand with considerable power.[1] Associations become actionable beliefs about a sport brand, which means that a brand's meaning is a measure of its muscle.

There are many ways a brand (and its elements) can be communicated to sport consumers. However, this communication typically falls under a programme of integrated marketing communications activities, whereby brand elements are nurtured and developed in order to bring about desirable and valuable associations between a sport brand and its target audience. To put it another way, the stuff that makes up a brand – like its products, attributes, and packaging – does not just accidentally assemble into cohesive representations that become symbols for sport enterprises. They are painstakingly crafted into signals, markers, and beacons for the kinds of ideas that the brand owners would like to exemplify. This book concerns such an endeavour – the process of branding sport. Getting this right is arguably the best investment a sport enterprise and its leaders can make.

A range of benefits can accrue to a sport, or its constituent elements, when its branding works well. These include improved perceptions of performance, greater customer loyalty, larger margins, increased marketing communications effectiveness, and additional brand extension opportunities. Such benefits can be measured by the concept of brand equity, or the goodwill attributable to a brand over and above its tangible assets.[2] When the mere mention of brand names of sporting titans such as Manchester United, Nike, the New York Yankees, or the Olympic Games can make the whole world sit up and take notice, you quickly grasp that a brand is far more than just the sum of its parts. In fact, you can begin to understand sport branding just by asking what those parts constitute – and realise that it is not that much! – at least relative to what some other corporate behemoths in the fast-moving consumer goods world or Silicon Valley can offer. There are no Los Angeles Lakers factories, nor guarded special recipes of FIFA World

Cups, nor powerful patents at FC Barcelona. What they all have, however, are unique, strong, and favourable connections to a multitude of fans whose life spirit is enmeshed with the characters of their sporting club and the brand it exudes. Those brands knit themselves with star athletes, iconic playing arenas, and an unnerving ability to shape a narrative of hope, ambition, and cultural significance that become enviable to all those other forms of business around them, itching for a share of the same sort of passion.[3]

Not only do sports and sport enterprises attempt to shape their own brands' symbolic characters, but they also try to leverage other brands to amplify the associations most desired. A sport may therefore benefit by using a brand or brand element associated with another organisation as a result of a commercial relationship with the other property, often in the form of a partnership or sponsorship. Naturally, the brands that flock to sponsor sport, or produce products associated with sport, stand to benefit also, provided they too get their branding right.

Strategically managing brand components in order to transform elements into a cohesive brand exemplifies the challenge of branding sport. Brand managers must be psychologists, curators, advertisers, and accountants all at once. When it all goes right, a sport brand, such as Real Madrid FC, the Dallas Cowboys, the Tour de France, and the New Zealand All Blacks can exhibit some of the most recognisable elements in the world, having moved towards an iconic status within business and popular culture. This is due to a combination of factors such as their longevity, global presence, resource investment, extensive integrated marketing communications efforts, sponsorship activities, and visibility. Consider, for example, how one of the world's leading sport footwear brands, adidas, has used stripe markings on their shoes and clothing for over 60 years. In so doing, they have reinforced awareness of this element and its placement on sportswear through extensive efforts over a sustained period, including the widespread sponsorship of athletes, teams, and events. The result is an intractable mark – stripes as it were – in the minds of sport consumers.

Why branding?

Let us proceed with the convention that in the broadest and simplest sense, a brand comprises a distinguishing name and symbol/s like logos, colours, and designs that serve to construct an identity that can be recognised amongst other offerings (themselves brands) in a competitive marketplace. As a result, a carefully constructed brand can signal to consumers that it stands for something more than the sum of its functional properties. And, when achieved, the signals stimulate consumers to retrieve powerful, often emotional, associations that they have embedded in their minds as a consequence of experience and repetition. But, why bother with all of this?

From a competitive perspective, sport enterprises are well advised to invest heavily in their branding strategy. In an increasingly competitive climate built around entertainment and disposable consumerism, sport enterprises must find ways to establish long-term connections with consumers that maintain value beyond a fleeting transaction. Branding offers the most effective method for cultivating sustainable relationships between brands and their users. In such ferocious environments where performances can ebb and flow on and off the field, the value inherent in a sport brand is the most resilient and long-lasting form of asset a sport enterprise can possess. A strong brand gives its owner a stable foundation of value that can weather poor seasons, new challenges, athletes that come and go, and rough markets.

At a more immediate level, successful branding demonstrably bolsters sales, profits, and reputation. In this respect, brand value provides a measurable indicator of consumer attraction to a brand, as well as loyalty and repeated purchases over time. It is also a proxy for consumer resilience when things go wrong. Finally, in environments like sport infused by tremendous competition, strong brand loyalty offers some insight into the likelihood that a consumer will defect to another brand. All brands seek a resistance to brand change in their consumers, especially because it can be expensive to keep up with new offerings from predatory competitors.

In the beginning

As early as the middle of the last century, the idea that a brand name could be more than just an identifying label was gaining popularity.[4] In fact, the key principle was already in motion, that a brand is a complex *symbol* with an essential character communicated by its words, imagery, and, most importantly, by an intangible suite of associations that build up over time as a result of being a public object. Although still nascent, even 65 years ago, the notion of a brand as a 'personality' was in play. Far more recently, it has become a foundation of contemporary marketing wherein elusive associations can be even more important than a product's functional performance.[5]

More elaborate interpretations of branding flourished in the post-war period heading into the socially looser 1960s. One pivotal work pushed the boundaries, declaring that in the new era of prosperity and growth, there was less concern with the concrete satisfactions of products based exclusively on function and utility, thereby opening the door to the symbolic significance of goods.[6] Increasingly, wealthy and bored buyers who had once been solely preoccupied with the practical value of products were gradually succumbing to a new motivation for consumption.

Instead of just what things could do, it was also about what they could evoke. The new way of looking at the world of consumption introduced the central idea that the experience of all products and services is indirect, mediated through associative objects, words, ideas, actions, and emotions. This suite of associations was also held within symbolic representations – the brands themselves – and was liberated when consumers came into contact with the symbolic forms that a brand expressed. That idea transformed branding and, doubtless, the entire world's experience of consumption. Brands represented products that were now psychological packages as much as physical ones. Symbols were more important than substances, as brands had wiggled their way into the minds and personal identities of consumers. People were becoming enamoured with brands far beyond the functional capabilities that a product or service could offer. A brand was a friend, a connection to a broader community, a reason to relate that went beyond the rational. For marketers and managers around the world, the result was a magical doorway into the hopes and dreams of consumers, a pathway that offered vast potential and redefined the concept of value.

Brands as value systems

In the 1980s and 1990s, the symbolic stocks of brands were fast on the rise. Accommodating the radical influence of brands as more than bundles of useful products and services, marketing commentators and researchers started to think about brand symbols from a value perspective.[7] Accordingly, textbooks moved to define a brand as a collection of symbols including names, designs, marks, and colours that enhanced the value of a product or service beyond their functional value.[8]

Over the course of another decade or so as organisations of all kinds, including sport, were hiring their first 'brand managers,' there was a marked upshift in granularity. From symbolic representation beyond function, the brand concept moved into more elaborate territory.[9] Symbols represented a brand, but they did not necessarily fully capture a brand's essence. Rather than the symbols, marketers were contemplating more about thinking and feeling.[10] It was less about what the symbols comprised and more about how they formed a meaning deep in the (relatively) inaccessible minds and memories of consumers.[11] The meanings consumers ascribed to brands became known as the brand image or brand attitude. While the terms image and attitude are relatively interchangeable in the branding world, they both capture the power of the brand. Image represents how a brand is viewed and the associations it is connected to. A brand's attitude is a more direct feeling of how those associations are combined and synergised. While for the purposes of an introduction to branding it is acceptable to think of brand image *or* brand attitude, the meaning that both terms convey should be melded to demonstrate the powerful force of value that is capable of being created through the associations that are both built and ascribed to by brands.

Symbols not only forge cognitive meanings, but also emotional ones. As an addition to the conceptual repertoire of brand managers, the leap into an emotional as well as cognitive domain proved decisive. There had been a shift from function to symbols to meaning, which meant that brands were understood as personal, virtually human, and were deeply engrained in consumers' psyches. It is from this foundation that we begin our sport branding insights.

Overview of the book

Sport Branding Insights explains how a sport brand goes beyond just an identifying badge, reinforced by a name or a logo that helps sport fans and consumers recognise a product or an organisation. It reveals how a brand becomes intrinsically linked with consumers' opinions and perceptions of a sport product and the organisation that owns it. Further, this book shows how the added value that a sport product possesses because of its brand name and identity heightens brand equity, or value. Readers will therefore come to understand how a powerful brand with high levels of equity that has both recognition in the market and strong associated imagery, can be created. Throughout, it demonstrates how the equity of a sporting brand can be enhanced by imbuing it with a spirit of the past through appeals to tradition, and by endowing it with human qualities of emotion, thought, and volition through the use of brand characters, colours, texts, and symbols. In short, this book offers a unique, concise, and easy-to-understand precis of a powerful, growing domain.

Section 1. Understanding Sport Brands introduces the key concepts of sport brands and branding in order to provide the reader with a foundational understanding of the domain. *Section 2. Building Sport Brands* works with the foundational concepts to explain how sport brands are constructed and what elements make up their constitution.

Section 3. Mobilising Sport Brands reveals how the elements of sport brands can be associated with consumer awareness, recognition, and, ultimately, a mental correlate. *Section 4. Leveraging Sport Brands* shows how consumer associations are transformed into equity and value with the aid of carefully fabricated and well-positioned marketing, advertising, and sponsorship. Finally, *Section 5. Reinventing Sport Brands* considers how branding translates into the contemporary reshaping of consumer approaches and brand value creation, as well as the auxiliary services available in the branding process that can prove useful in navigating the complexity of messaging. Next, we introduce some key concepts and definitions in order to locate the branding process within the wider schema of marketing.

Notes

1 Stewart, B., Smith, A., & Nicholson, M. (2003). Sport consumer typologies: A critical review. *Sport Marketing Quarterly, 12*(4), 206–216.
2 Lassar, W., Mittal, B., & Sharma, A. (1995). Measuring customer-based brand equity. *Journal of Consumer Marketing, 12*(4), 11–19.
3 Smith, A.C.T., Stavros, C., & Westberg, K. (2017). *Brand Fans.* Cham: Springer.
4 Gardner, B.G., & Levy, S.J. (1955). The product and the brand. *Harvard Business Review, 33* (March–April), 33–39.
5 Aaker, J.L. (1997). Dimensions of brand personality. *Journal of Marketing Research, 34*(3), 347–356.
6 Levy, S.J. (1959). Symbols for sale. *Harvard Business Review, 37* (March–April), 117–124.
7 de Chernatony, L., & Dall'Olmo R.F. (1998). Defining a brand: Beyond the literature with expert interpretations. *Journal of Marketing Management, 14*, 417–443.
8 Farquhar, P. (1989). Managing brand equity. *Marketing Research, 1* (September), 24–33.
9 Keller, K.L. (2003). Brand synthesis: The multidimensionality of brand knowledge. *Journal of Consumer Research, 29*, 596–600.
10 Stern, B.B. (2006). What does brand mean? Historical-analysis method and construct definition. *Journal of the Academy of Marketing Science, 34*(2), 216–233.
11 Aaker, D. (1996). *Building Strong Brands.* New York: Free Press.

1 Understanding sport brands

Introduction – key concepts

When the renowned professional English football club, Leeds United, announced a change to their club crest in early 2018, it was met with such uproar – including over 77,000 signatures on a petition – that they abandoned the idea within hours of announcing it. The badge, which featured what was termed a 'Leeds Salute' (an image of a person placing a clenched fist across their chest), carried associated wording that read 'celebrating fans at the heart of our community.' Unfortunately, many of those fans who were being celebrated viewed the new design as 'awful,' 'shocking,' and 'horrendous.'[1] What was ostensibly a well-intentioned 'image' for the club was met with disdain when revealed, despite the club launching the design in a tweet that boasted of '6 months of research' with '10,000 people consulted.' The image was emotionally visceral to many fans who attach themselves to the club from cradle to grave, and see every branding touchpoint as something sacred. Leeds United subsequently launched a campaign to fan-source a new crest, and quickly received over 1,200 submissions as a result.

A brand, in its simplest form, can be seen as an identifying badge – reinforced, leveraged, amplified, and mobilised by device marks, or the suite of images, words, or logos that help consumers recognise a product or an organisation. As a result, a sport brand becomes intractably linked with consumers' opinions and perceptions – something that Leeds' well-meaning management discovered.

A carefully constructed and curated sport brand will do much more than merely provide ready identification. It will urge sport consumers to think of the brand in terms of its relationship to other sport brands, usually competitors, in a marketing process known as positioning. Because branding and positioning are connected, we will later explain how the entire enactment of sport branding must be reflective of a thoughtful positioning strategy. For example, it would be counterproductive to brand a new product as a luxury item when it is positioned in a low-cost category.

Another factor that we need to introduce now is that sport product sales can be affected by how easily a consumer can tell different products apart. Branding takes on a particular importance towards what marketer's call 'differentiation,' or the related concept of 'distinctiveness,' because it offers a potent way for products and other brand elements to stand out from all the rest.[2] Standing out goes well beyond just having a different name, colour scheme, or logo. Branding sport gives consumers a reason to create associations with the brand, which become reinforced over time. Branding is therefore a way of augmenting a product by helping to create associated ideas that make it different in powerful, enduring ways. The added value that a product possesses because of its brand name and identity is called brand equity.[3] The concept of equity is critical in branding as it ultimately provides a barometer of success.

All the previous leads to our following definitions. A sport brand is the symbolic representation of everything that a sport enterprise or organisation seeks to stand for, leading to expectations about its value and performance. A brand can be portrayed as an identifying badge that triggers consumers to remember a product or an organisation. It can be a name, a design, a symbol (or logo), an image, or a combination of these things. By extension, sport branding is the process used to help elements and products stand out from the crowd by positioning them through associated ideas and concepts.

Sport marketing

Branding falls under the broader activities of sport marketing, which encompasses all the planning and implementing activities designed to meet the needs or desires of customers. Sport marketing pays attention to the development of a product and to its pricing, promotion, and distribution. It aims to create an exchange, where the customer gives up something (usually money) for a product or service they believe is of equal or greater value. Although the term 'product' directly refers to tangible items, it is quite common to use it to represent the entire offering to consumers, including services. Thus, it is conventional to speak of the 'sport product' in a global sense as a representative term for all offerings associated with sport, whether in physical form like sport equipment, or as a service such as entertainment. Sport marketing aims to not only entice people to try products or services but also keep them as long-term customers.[4]

For reference, the American Marketing Association defines marketing as '... *the activity, set of institutions, and processes for creating, communicating, delivering, and exchanging offerings that have value for customers, clients, partners, and society at large.*'[5] That is, every marketer is required to focus on the strategic processes an organisation undertakes, or could undertake, to allow it to successfully satisfy the identified wants and/or needs of its target audiences. The motivations, desires, perceptions, and actions of these audiences are critical, as the central tenet of marketing is an exchange. A marketer attempts to bring about a profitable exchange by managing a 'mix' of product, promotion, pricing, and distribution elements, which collectively comprise the basic tools of marketing. The concept of 'mix' is critically important as it highlights the interconnected and synergistic approach marketing seeks.

Since we are all relentlessly exposed to its effects, the term 'marketing' has universal currency, although it may be used in different ways. Marketing is seen by some as the use of advertising, publicity, and personal selling techniques to make consumers aware of a product, or to attract more consumers to buy it. For some, it is all about making a sale.

In reality, sport marketing's influence has far greater reach than this narrow and mechanistic interpretation suggests. However, we can start with an uncontroversial point in that marketing, in general, is all about satisfying the needs of consumers. Sport marketing, therefore, revolves around meeting the needs of sport consumers, including: people who watch and play sport; download and stream programmes; buy merchandise; collect memorabilia; purchase sports goods such as clothing and shoes; 'surf' sport-related websites to find out the latest gossip surrounding their favourite team, player, or event; or even participate in esports.

Sport marketing can be applied across two dimensions. First, it involves the application of marketing concepts to sport products and services, and second, it involves the marketing of non-sport, or tangentially related products, through an association to sport. The first dimension involves the application of general marketing practices to sport-related products and services. The second dimension encompasses the marketing of other consumer and industrial products or services through sport. Sport is therefore first a marketable commodity, and second a platform for other brands to connect to, given its power as a cultural and social medium. This juxtaposition of sport as object and medium is a complicating factor in its marketing, bringing both enormous opportunities and challenges as sporting brands try and offer pure experiences that are inevitably commercialised through a desire to remain competitive and to maximise revenues.

In summary, sport marketing involves the marketing *of* sport, and marketing *through* sport. The marketing of sport products and services directly to sport consumers can include sporting equipment, professional competitions, sport events, local club or team advertising, designing publicity stunts to promote athletes, selling season tickets, and developing licensed apparel for sale. Marketing through sport occurs when a non-sport, or tangentially related product, is marketed through an association to sport, like a professional athlete endorsing a breakfast cereal, a financial-services business sponsoring a tennis tournament, or a beer company securing exclusive rights to provide its products at a sporting venue.

Sport marketing to sport branding

Like any form of marketing, sport marketing seeks to fulfil the needs and wants of consumers through the provision of sport services and sport-related products. However, sport marketing deviates from conventional marketing in that it also has the ability to encourage the consumption of non-sport products and services by association. As we noted earlier, sport marketing means both the marketing of sport itself, and the use of sport as a tool to market other products and services. These twin aspects of sport marketing have a material effect on sport brands because branding relies on the successful cultivation of associations.

Well before anything can be sold to a sport consumer, a sport product must secure a place in the mind of that consumer in a favourable way. The process of cultivating such a response lies at the heart of branding, and when a sport brand has grasped a firm place in consumers' minds, then it may be considered 'positioned,' a concept we shall describe in detail shortly. The consequence of successful branding and the acquisition of strong market positioning is not merely a single transaction. Rather, sport marketing reflects the establishment of an ongoing relationship between a sport brand and its users. Such a relationship is an essential part of all branding, allowing communities to form around brands, bringing a multitude of benefits, including loyalty, along with it.[6]

For our purposes, we shall consider sport marketing to be the process of planning how a sport brand is positioned and how the delivery of its products or services is to be implemented in order to establish a relationship between a sport brand and its consumers.

The marketing of sport may appear at first to be similar to general marketing, but the two can diverge. For example, the sport product is often highly inconsistent and unpredictable because it is not possible to predict the outcome of a sporting match or control the quality of play. In many other industries, the failure to guarantee the quality of a product would be disastrous. Another significant difference is that few products can evoke the emotional attachment and personal identification that sport commands. Although such nuances do not necessarily make sport marketing categorically different from general marketing, in order to create a potent sport brand, the unique circumstances of the sport marketplace and its consumers must remain the sovereign concern.[7] For the most part, a customised sport branding response builds upon the foundation established by what marketers call integrated marketing communications.

Integrated marketing communications

Marketing communication comprises a broad process through which sport brands form shared meanings with their target audiences. Integration is achieved through an array of measures like public relations, sales promotions, personal selling, and advertising, each of which seeks to form part of a 'jigsaw puzzle' in the minds of consumers as they put together experiences and knowledge to develop both awareness of a brand and then a specific image of it (or attitude towards it). Every action a brand takes – whether planned or not – sends a message that a potential consumer may use to deduce information.[8] As a result, the 'integration' of messages to consumers proves essential to ensure a synergy in the form of uniformity, consistency, and positive resonance. In order to achieve a branding strategy based on integrated marketing communications, brand managers need to start with an understanding of consumer and fan behaviour.

Consumer and fan behaviour

As we have previously explained, brand associations form the critical core of sport branding as they relate directly to the identification and evaluation process used by fans and consumers. Through experience, sport consumers identify 'cues' and formulate learning behaviours to assist in making purchasing decisions. Cues provide a stimulus, which may be thought of as heuristics, or approaches to problem-solving that seek acceptable solutions through a kind of 'short-cut.'[9]

Heuristics do not need to provide 'correct' results, but merely a decision-making process or solution that seems plausible and helpful to a sport consumer. For example, in a blind taste-test of an energy drink, a researcher may place the identical product into two containers but differentiate them with labels suggesting that one is a premium, well-known 'brand' associated with an active sport such as snowboarding, while the other is a cheaper unbranded version with no external connections. A consumer in this situation may expect – and then confirm after tasting – that the container with the well-known brand name is superior based on a well-worn heuristic that reminds them that premium brands are usually better quality than cheaper alternatives, or even that the association to snowboarding suggests a positive element, raising it above the other brand.

When moving through a (relatively) rational decision-making process, a consumer typically moves through five stages towards an escalating level of purchasing urgency.[10] These stages will be revisited in more detail later in this book.

1　Category need – this stage of the buying process involves acknowledgement of a discrepancy between an actual and a desired state.
2　Information search – consumers aware of a discrepancy search for solutions, and this may involve mental and/or physical search processes.
3　Evaluation of alternatives – having searched for options, a consumer will then evaluate the alternatives, seeking to prioritise those most suitable based upon their needs.
4　Purchase decision – having evaluated, a consumer then makes a choice, which may include the product and also where it is purchased from.
5　Post-purchase behaviour – the period following purchase is important as it provides consumers with an opportunity to consider their purchase relative to their goals and expectations, and will form the basis for future decisions in the category.

Advertising

Another concept worth exploring at this early stage should be familiar to most readers, and as noted, entails a key element of integrated marketing communications. Advertising contributes to marketing and sport branding in that it represents a planned and directed form of message exposure between a brand and its target audience(s). It therefore offers a key bridge between a brand and its potential purchasers given the meaning transfer that can occur as a purposeful result of its transmission.[11] Advertising works to persuade, inform, and remind sport consumers about the key features of brand elements, on the assumption that repeated exposure leads to strong associations. Advertising can take numerous forms and retains a preeminent role in integrated marketing communications, especially with the emergence of new media platforms that provide novel avenues for reaching and influencing target audiences. While people may question the traditional platforms, such as television, upon which the concept of advertising achieved worldwide significance, the newer and emerging platforms do nothing to dissipate the value and power of advertising as a tool for marketers. Indeed, with metrics ramping up in precision as consumers leave digital footprints wherever they traverse, the concept of advertising is more nuanced, more impactful, more surgical, and more diverse than ever before.

Target audiences

A keen reader might have already observed that this book speaks of 'target audiences' rather than 'target markets.' This is a critical distinction in the world of branding. The concept of target markets is long associated with a sales and selling mentality that looks upon the market as a relatively inanimate 'thing.' A market in our terms is a category or space where exchanges can occur. While that market-space is important, what matters more is the audience within it and how each grouping that may exist is addressed to form the correct levels of communication that will permit brand knowledge to grow. In many sport markets, the audiences are vast and complex, ranging from rusted-on fans to grant-giving governments, stakeholders such as sponsors, and even other teams within a league. For a sport brand to thrive, it needs to be able to connect with all of these audiences. While a strong, resilient brand can appear as one to all of them, the level of connection and communication that will occur at each audience level will need fine-tuning and careful consideration. A brand can mean something similar to many types of people; just look at the broad success of Apple, McDonald's, and Toyota. Yet, the micro-management required to form a relationship to all the different audiences goes well beyond a single, unifying message.

Conclusion – from elements to associations

To recap, a sport brand can be many things, including a name, a design, a symbol, an image, or even a combination of these. A brand name and a brand mark (or logo) are two of the most common representations of a brand. A brand name is a word, a written label, or even group of letters and/or numbers; it is usually something that can be verbalised rather than merely an image. The choice of brand name will communicate (or symbolise) a unique idea. For example, some brand names might suggest strength and confidence, like the Titans – the American football team based in the state of Tennessee – while others might suggest boldness, like Nike, the goddess of victory in Greek mythology. If you do not agree with these connotations, it means that you hold a different brand identity in your mind. The correct meaning is always the one in the mind of the consumer, as they never arrange the puzzle pieces of marketing incorrectly. It can only be the marketer who has erred if the sum of their efforts fails to make the desired impact on a consumer or the target audience to which they belong. Therefore, the importance of branding is paramount. It is a game within a game, in the world of sport.

Brands can help consumers to remember sport enterprises and their product offerings and can stimulate resonant images in their minds. A powerful brand has both a high level of awareness in the market and a strong associated imagery. It can literally be the difference between failing indifference and spectacular success.

Notes

1 BBC (2018). *Leeds United: Club delays introduction of new crest until 2019–20 season.* Retrieved from https://www.bbc.com/sport/football/ 43157773.
2 Romaniuk, J., Sharp, B., & Ehrenberg, A. (2007). Evidence concerning the importance of perceived brand differentiation. *Australasian Marketing Journal, 15*(2), 42–54.
3 Aaker, D. (1996). *Building Strong Brands.* New York: Free Press.
4 Smith. A.C.T. (2008). *Introduction to Sport Marketing.* Burlington, NJ: Butterworth-Heinemann.
5 American Marketing Association (n.d.). *Definitions of marketing.* Retrieved from https://www.ama.org/AboutAMA/Pages/Definition-of-Marketing. aspx.
6 Muniz Jr., A.M., & O'Guinn, T.C. (2001). Brand community. *Journal of Consumer Research, 27*(4), 412–432.
7 Smith, A.C.T., & Stewart, B. (2010). The special features of sport: A critical revisit. *Sport Management Review, 13*(1), 1–13.
8 Schultz, D.E., & Schultz, H.F. (1998). Transitioning marketing communication into the twenty-first century. *Journal of Marketing Communications, 4*(1), 9–26.
9 Gigerenzer, G., & Gaissmaier, W. (2011). Heuristic decision making. *Annual Review of Psychology, 62,* 451–482.
10 Engel, J.F., Blackwell, R.D., & Kollat, D.T. (1978). *Consumer Behavior.* Hinsdale, IL: Dryden Press.
11 Meenaghan, T. (1995). The role of advertising in brand image development. *Journal of Product & Brand Management, 4*(4), 23–34.

2 Building sport brands

Introduction – What is a sport brand?

It is not uncommon for a goal-scoring footballer or century-making cricketer to kiss the nearest sporting emblem that resides on their clothing. This literal affection towards the sports brand they represent is emblematic of a display of love and pride for the 'tribe' – a symbolism of unity and passion that extends beyond the rational and into the emotional.

The time has come to venture into more depth about what a sport brand comprises, keeping in mind a broader aim of laying the foundations essential to building such a brand. To answer this deceptively simple question we will outline a basic definition of a sport brand, discuss a variety of brand elements which can constitute (separately or together) a brand, and expand on the concept of a brand with a more detailed analysis of how brand elements are ascribed value by sport consumers.

Recall that we started at a relatively superficial level by describing a brand as a name, term, symbol, sign, design, or combination of these elements. The collective of these elements identifies a product to consumers by differentiating it from the product offerings of competitors. Irrespective of this identification role, a brand derives its relevance, and therefore its impact, from the relationship between the elements and associations formed by consumers.

A brand should not be confused with a product. A product can be seen as a functional offering, be it a good or a service. A product satisfies the basic needs and wants of consumers. For example, a desire for rehydration may be delivered by a number of products such as water, juice, or energy drinks. Many brands compete in these product categories, and while they may offer similar, or in some cases, identical forms of need/want satisfaction to each other, they do so under the auspices of a brand and the inferences that accompany it. A 'brand is therefore a product, but one that adds other dimensions that differentiate it in some way from other products designed to satisfy the same need.'[1] For example, sporting footwear can be viewed as the product, but Reebok is viewed as the branded product, and thus will carry with it any elements that the company has been able to instil in the shared meaning of its brand over years of consumer use, marketing communication, and other interactions.

Taking a further step, sport branding goes beyond mere identification and involves a complex set of relationships between organisations and their audiences. In this way, sport brands are not 'owned' (in the marketing sense, not the legal sense) by organisations, but by consumers. It is the meaning in consumers' minds that has evolved through learning and experience that creates brand value. For example, leading scholars such as Keller speak of a brand as a product plus a collection of rational, emotional, tangible, and intangible elements,[2] Aaker describes a brand as a 'mental box' in the consumer's head,[3] and Kapferer indicates that a brand is '...a summary of unique values and benefits.'[4] The value of a brand is determined by the degree to which consumers recognise it and consequently experience an emotional response. Together, these elements are often called brand knowledge,[5] which consists of two important concepts: brand awareness and brand attitude.

Brand awareness is typically measured by the ability of a sport consumer to identify a brand in sufficient detail to make a purchase. Brand attitude, which will logically come as a consequence of brand awareness, may be thought of as a sport consumer's thoughts and feelings, or overall evaluation of a brand in relation to its ability to meet the motivations that exist for purchase. A consumer's attitude to a brand may vary over time and will be influenced by a range of factors, including previous experiences with the brand, such as word-of-mouth, advertising, and point-of-sale promotional material.

The 'branding' concept

As we have suggested, most theorists and practitioners define a brand as a set of complex offerings and associations that take shape in the minds of consumers, and subsequently play out through market economics. To repeat the important foundational premise, at its most basic level, a brand is a name, symbol, or design, or combination of these elements, which identifies a product to consumers by differentiating it from the product offerings of competitors. As we have foreshadowed, however, sport branding has come to mean much more than this.

The true value of a brand to the sport organisation that owns or controls it resides in its collective psychological and behavioural effects. Associative effects tied up in a brand's meaning and symbols influence how and why sport consumers make decisions, especially with regard to perceived value, product identification, risk reduction, and buying process evaluation. Consumers infer such associations – that evolve over time and after sustained, strategic, and integrated efforts – by brands to manage the brand-to-consumer relationship. Strong, resilient brands may take many years to acquire positive associations and do not come about through fortune or accident. Rather, positive brand associations take form through a learning process that consumers experience as a result of exposure to integrated marketing communications programmes, which transpire over a sustained period.

Sporting brands are some of the oldest brands in existence. The Melbourne Football Club plays in the Australian Football League, and is one of the world's oldest professional clubs of any football code, dating back to 1858. The 'modern' Olympic Games began in 1896, and even relative newcomers like the New York Giants of the National Football League (NFL) in the USA date back to 1925. That is not to say that longevity is a key to branding success, but it certainly plays a part. Even relatively new and highly successful brands in the world of fast-moving technology, like Apple and Microsoft, took decades to really thrive and catapult themselves to sustained success.

A central tenet of branding holds that consumers forge relationships with the more intangible brand image rather than with the more material products or services that those brands represent.[6] Kevin Roberts, a renowned advertising executive, wrote a book entitled *Lovemarks*, triumphing the strong emotional attachments fashioned between consumers and some exclusive luxury brands.[7] Roberts' concept of 'lovemarks' resiles from the more common contemporary phenomenon where most products in a category offer basically identical core benefits. Sport brands seem to exemplify the 'lovemarks' factor, forming strong and passionate connections with fans that are often visibly displayed, aggressively defended, and passed on from generation to generation. Curiously, despite the fact that two teams in the same sporting competition offer exactly the same product benefits, no fans of either would consider switching, as the value proposition for each brand remains steadfastly independent. As a result, in sport branding, the difference between products and their custodian brands can be immense. There are few product brands that can impart such loyalty. While a fan of the English Premier League's Arsenal FC is likely to change everything, from toothpaste brands to car brands, and possibly even spouses in their lifetime, it is unlikely that they will cease being a fan of the 'Gunners' for any reason, even if they left London and moved overseas.

A brand encompasses much more than just an exchange around a product. Brands include other dimensions that have been added to the core product in order to differentiate them from other products designed to satisfy the same needs. Differences may be intangible or tangible.[8] When sport consumers buy a brand, they purchase more than just the physical product. Consumers also purchase all the associations that a brand embodies, such as entertainment, social success, hope, distraction, identification, meaning, and vicarious experience.

Building a strong sport brand can be a complicated and difficult task due to factors like a crowded competitive arena, fragmentation of markets, complex brand strategies including dynamic digital and social media channels, and the unrelenting pressure to compete on price.[9] Consider, for example, that the congested football (soccer) market in Greater London comprises 11 professional teams, of which six compete in the English Premier League and five in the Football League. At the same time, around 200 amateur clubs play in various local and regional leagues. Given the difficulty in building a sport brand at all, the achievement of a strong brand constitutes a rich and valuable asset to sport enterprises that have been able to convert favourable associations into value. This value from a branding perspective is referred to as brand equity.

Brand equity

Brand associations have value because they materially influence consumer purchasing behaviour, and, of course, more sales mean greater economic value.[10] Beyond the immediate economic return, however, brand equity reflects a stock of capital of as yet unrealised future sales. As such, brand equity may be the most valuable asset that a sporting enterprise might possess. It has, as a consequence, emerged as a highly popular bottom-line measure of marketing success.[11]

Brand equity can be thought of as a proxy for a brand's value because it provides '…marketers with a vital strategic bridge from their past to their future.'[12] It also has the advantage of describing the marketing effects uniquely attributable to a brand as it materialises as 'a set of assets (and liabilities)… that add to (or subtract from) the value provided by a product or service to a firm and/or to that firm's customers.'[13] Just as your bank account depicts the status of your personal equity, so does brand equity signal the health of a brand.

Brand equity can be revealed in numerous ways, but perhaps the most important is demonstrated in the way consumers respond to a brand's marketing and communication efforts. Positive equity suggests that sport consumers react more favourably to a product and its marketing when it is identified rather than when it remains anonymous. For example, when faced with a choice of bottled water from a leading brand, such as Evian, and with a brand from an unknown manufacturer, a thirsty gym exerciser who chooses the Evian brand is also expressing a positive appreciation for the brand. Its value to them is therefore more than the sum of the bottle's contents. A consumer's feelings may stem from experience, advertising messages, or symbolic associations with the brand elements, including, for example, the classy French-sounding name, imagery invoking the pristine freshness of pure alpine waters, or a combination as illustrated by the distinctive label. If another water brand were to come along, however, it could analyse the gym exerciser market and note that Evian's broader appeal as a premium water might not be optimised to such a segment. A product such as 'Pump,' a brand in Australia and New Zealand offered by Coca-Cola Amatil, might then appear, featuring not only an apt gym name, but with features such as a push-out lid for easy consumption when moving, and a sturdy shape that appeals to those users who are keen to associate all their products with their health-enriching lifestyle. For Coca-Cola Amatil, perhaps better known for its sugary products, a brand like Pump allows it to build its broader equity by targeting specific brands to specific markets in ways that create positive outcomes.

Going another step, it is possible to distinguish between corporate brand equity and brand-item equity. Corporate equity relates to the overall value of a corporate brand at the macro level. Although sport organisations might not be traditionally viewed as 'corporations,' the reality remains that corporate entities dominate any list of the world's most prominent sporting brands, notable companies including Nike, Manchester United, ESPN, Formula 1 Motor Racing, the Indian Premier League Twenty20 cricket, and the Red Bull energy drink manufacturer. It should be remembered that brand equity is of concern to sport organisations at both the macro and the micro levels.

Prominent sport sponsor, Coca-Cola, presents an apt depiction of brand-item and corporate equity. On its own, Coca-Cola as one of the world's most valuable brands, can establish brand-item equity that confers the brand with a valuation of US$73 billion, simply based on the goodwill the brand has gathered as one of the most recognisable and desired products on the planet.[14] This impacts consumer choice, and the strength the brand commands to set premium prices for its products. A company like Coca-Cola, moving to the corporate equity level, also comprises in its various markets and divisions around the world a series of brands (e.g., Sprite, Dasani, Minute Maid, Powerade) that compete within different sub-markets or categories. The brand-item equity of these brands can also be measured at an individual or micro level based on their performance within a given sub-market or category of goods, and is of more direct relevance and impact to marketing managers because it relates directly to their day-to-day activities, including sales, competitors, and budgets. As of 2019, The Coca-Cola Company has a market capitalisation of around US$200 billion. This number reflects the total value of its public shares and reflects its corporate equity and strength.

Positive brand equity implies that consumers are familiar with a brand and that favourable, strong, and unique associations are stored in their memories; associations drive perceptions and preferences in ways that are of value to the brand owner. A brand's equity is thus determined by whether sport consumers know a brand, and, as a result, by what consumers know or perceive about the brand in terms of its elements. An understanding of a brand's elements culminates in what we have termed 'brand knowledge,' or the combination of brand awareness and brand attitude. We shall return to the important concept of brand knowledge in more detail later, following further explanation about brand elements.

Brand elements

Towards the objective of building a brand, marketers must evaluate numerous options in the selection and combination of brand elements that work to best display, identify, and differentiate their products. Elements can be evaluated on the basis of several key criteria, central amongst which are memorability, meaningfulness, transferability, likeability, adaptability, and protectability.[15]

Individual brand elements, or a combination of a suite of elements, comprise the building blocks of a brand's identity, its image, and ultimately its equity. Without brand elements, products become commodities; the value associated with any uniqueness dissipates without a cohesive and identifying symbolic marker to signal to consumers that consumption has greater meaning than a simple exchange. For example, sport fans rarely seek nothing more than to just watch a game and go home. In fact, often it is more a matter of supporting a particular team – a brand – than merely paying for the opportunity to be entertained for an afternoon. The key point to remember is that brand elements will only prove valuable to a brand owner if they establish positive associations with consumers and contribute to the equity, or overall value, of a brand. As a result, brand associations can occur individually with brand elements or as some combination or permutation of these elements.

Creating brand associations

Brand associations are critical in sport branding as they relate directly to the identification and evaluation process used by consumers. For example, a shopper in a retail environment will more likely choose products for which they can recognise some positive characteristic, like a symbol indicating that it was made in the country of sale, or one specifying a particularly attractive constituent or ingredient. Thus, brand elements are critical to the success of sport brands as they swiftly and reliably capture and reproduce the key associations of a product. A flash of a logo, part of a jingle, a colour, the shape of a package, and so forth may instantly convey characteristics of the brand to consumers. We shall now go through a series of ways in which brand associations can be wielded to link with brand elements.

First, associations may be formed on the basis of a product's name. For example, apparel and sport fashion brand 'Billabong,' a uniquely Australian term for a body of water, was founded on Australia's Gold Coast, and has maintained a strong connotation with Australian beach culture and imagery, despite being absorbed into the ownership of bigger organisations with global headquarters as well as ambitions. These associations positively affect the perceptions of products that are worn by individuals for whom they resonate in terms of personal identity, suggesting that the associated benefits are transferred from the beach lifestyle to the products.

Second, associations may be linked to a distinctive logo, such as that of Ralph Lauren (polo player on horseback), that appears on an otherwise plain shirt, and thus instils that piece of clothing with a sense of style, and ultimately the wearer with a sense of confidence or achievement. In this case, the sophistication and exclusivity of a sport that is associated with wealthy audiences.

Third, associations may be established through a character or spokesperson who appears in the advertising or on the packaging of the product. Examples include cartoon characters who may be seen

on products like energy drinks in order to depict larger-than-life outcomes inferred as a result of consuming the product. Similarly, the
solid, black leaping puma on the eponymous footwear brand has come
to represent strength, activity, and speed.

Fourth, associations may arise via a co-branded endorsement logo,
such as the Australian Heart Foundation's 'Tick,' which signals a credi-
ble and authentic level of healthiness to consumers. Other examples include Blackberry with Porsche, as well as Nike with Apple. Co-branding
offers several compelling advantages because it can introduce products
of one brand to another, enhance and elevate the image of both brands,
and permanently change brand perceptions through mutually positive
associations, or what are sometimes called 'spill-over effects.'

Fifth, associations can be influenced by the use of colour in order
to establish psychological effects, social identification, or aesthetic
impact. As a result, some brands become intrinsically inseparable
from their colour schematic, like Ferrari's distinctive blazing red, the
Los Angeles Laker's purple script, and the dark blue of the New York
Yankees. Colour is a particularly important brand element in sport as
it symbolises the tribal nature of fandom. For many sport marketers,
the choice of colour, should they get to decide it, may prove one of the
most important branding decisions they make. It can also lead to su-
perstition, with the NFL's Denver Broncos apparently shunning their
traditional orange uniform for the 2016 Super Bowl to play in white,
given their 0–4 record in Super Bowls where they wore their traditional shirts[16] – (for the record, the white-wearing Broncos won that
Super Bowl, defeating the Carolina Panthers 24–10). For their part,
the relatively new Panthers (established in 1993) wore predominantly
black, a colour chosen when they were formed, in part, for the merchandise opportunities it offers, with dark clothing being particularly
appealing to a wide range of fashion-conscious fans.

The mind of the consumer

Brand associations reflect how concepts become arranged in consumers'
short- and long-term memories, especially when they are anchored with
weighty rational and/or emotional elements. Leading Australian market
researcher Max Sutherland draws an excellent analogy for brand association and attitude by asking people to calculate how many windows are
in their homes.[17] The task typically 'forces' people to project themselves
mentally into their homes and progressively move from room to room
to come up with the answer. Sutherland thinks that such a retrieval process is typical of consumer product brand associations because we link

various bits of previously unconnected information in our minds to arrive at feelings and attitudes towards brands and products.

In sport branding, the journey into consumers' minds is particularly complex given the various factors that drive their thinking (literally) are incredibly nuanced and reflective of a range of internal and external factors. A child, for example, will almost certainly have their sporting relationships influenced by simple geographical factors. A boy in Japan may develop an interest in Sumo wrestling, while a girl in Ireland may be passionate about Gaelic football, each one thanks to nothing more than the influence of location. Modern technology is now making such distinctions blurrier, with many living in warm climates outside of Canada becoming fans of the National Hockey League (NHL), while those in landlocked countries may develop an appreciation for the sport of surfing and the lifestyle branding it espouses.

Aside from the increasingly irrelevant aspect of geography, it is possible to classify how people become sport fans across three elements: psychological motives, sociocultural motives, and self-concept motives.[18] Psychological motives stem from a variety of impulses that consumers have to satisfy internal needs. These can range from seeking a form of stimulation or excitement, an escape from the mundane or the monotony of existence, the feeling of aesthetic pleasure that sport can bring, and the inherent and largely unpredictably drama and entertainment that unfolds in sport. In many ways, these psychological concepts can be encapsulated by the concept of eustress,[19] a critical concept to fandom that is typically not well understood by brand managers as creating stress in customers seems counterintuitive.

Eustress, which has been positively correlated to well-being and satisfaction in life, is a form of positive stress that comes through the presence of a challenge, interlaced with hope and ambition.[20] Participating in sport, such as entering a local tennis tournament, watching your child play soccer, or cheering your team in the playoffs, can all stimulate eustress. It arrives as a biochemical reaction that serves as a powerful stimulant to the psychological elements of sport. Brands in sport can target eustress by deploying dramatic elements to signal the challenge ahead, the threat of danger, or the hope and satisfaction of a potential victory. Fans can feel an enormous stress in a sporting match, particularly if the event ebbs and flows towards different outcomes. That fans willingly commit themselves to this form of stress speaks to the special relationship that sport brands can develop with their fans and how eustress, as opposed to distress or stress, can be harvested beneficially.

While sociocultural factors such as family and social interaction, cultural connections, and economic benefits are all key motivators, sport brands also readily tap into the self-concept motives of fans by highlighting belonging and group affiliation, the tribal connections inherent in sport, and the concept of vicarious achievement that can arise. Sport brands exploit these motives by providing brand elements that fans can readily associate with. In-so-doing, brands recognise that such connections can bring favourable outcomes that are beneficial both internally in terms of happiness and accomplishment, as well as within consumers' broader lives by feeling connected to society on a shared journey of achievement and support.

In the case of some brands, associations may be founded on just a few key brand identity elements. For example, Coca-Cola's distinct bottle shape sparks the positive associations the brand has built up with regard to fun and enjoyment; the five-coloured interlinking Olympic rings signify passion and humanity; the University of Notre Dame's green 'Fighting Irish' leprechaun signals the historical significance and pride of a school renowned for its overachieving American football team; Liverpool's spine-tingling rendition of the song 'You'll Never Walk Alone' leaves fans (and sometimes opponents) in tears of joy and shared spirit; and, the NHL's shield speaks to history and accomplishment in a notoriously combative and competitive sport. All represent significant and powerful brand elements on their own, even though the 'brand experience' when purchasing or consuming such products may comprise much more than just one brand element.

Brand elements can operate by themselves or in combination to communicate with target audiences. For example, in sport branding, it is common for sponsors and sport properties to align colours and imagery. Puma and the Brooklyn Nets share a solemn livery of black and white, for instance, while Ikea and the University of Michigan both utilise similar versions of blue and yellow (or 'maize' as the university prefers to refer to the colour) to dramatic visual effect. Also, Pepsi's distinctive red, white, and blue beach ball logo and the Montreal Expos' emblem each depicts a spirit and swirls.

Certain brand elements might be more important to certain sport consumers, dependent upon their experiences, behaviours, and buying processes. As an example, in the case of sports footwear, and more specifically Nike, the brand logo is particularly relevant not only because of the role logos play in footwear identification, but also due to the way the company has used the singular element to distinguish itself. Few sporting fans could see the famous 'swoosh' and not think of Nike, and from there the array of talent from Michael Jordan to Serena Williams who have come to symbolise the 'brand in action.'

As the number, scope, and style of element associations will vary considerably by market situation, product category, and strategic focus, there is no definitive list of what can be characterised as a brand element. However, the following are all examples of brand elements, which we will consider next: logos and symbols, brand names and URLs, characters and spokespeople, slogans and jingles, packaging (including colour), and creative style. It is these elements, when appropriately activated, that form the foundation of a brand in a tangible sense, and which can then be built on through intangible associations that can create lasting value and connection.

Logos and symbols

Often related to the brand name is a graphical element or symbol typically referred to as the 'brand logo.' It provides a shorthand, visual representation of a brand and can be used with or without a brand name. In fact, sometimes a logo can become so ubiquitous as to gain fame and recognition simply by standing alone. Examples include the Olympic rings, Nike's 'Swoosh,' and Ferrari's prancing horse, all of which are arguably just as famous as McDonald's golden arches in consumer culture.

For the most part, the terms brand logo and brand symbol are used interchangeably. Technically speaking, logos can encompass wide-ranging designs, from a brand name written in distinctive form, such as Coca-Cola, Google, and EA Sports, through to abstract designs such as the relatively new Paralympic Games logo of three 'Agitos,' coloured red, blue, and green,[21] and those somewhere in between like the New York Yankees 'Y' superimposed on the 'N,' and the Dallas Cowboys blue and white star. Logos absent of words are technically symbols.[22]

To the passing observer, logos and symbols tend not to be seen as brand elements so much as the brand itself. While sport brands comprise numerous elements, an enormous emphasis is placed on the logo or symbol a brand employs. Given the power of logos and symbols to wordlessly express an entire brand's identity in the form of an immediate and instantly recognisable visual cue, the importance should not be too surprising. For strong brands, the logo or symbol they display presents the very embodiment of its identity to sport consumers; after all, the image has been expressly created to reflect the personality of the brand, and has usually been crafted from 'scratch.' In some cases, within sport, the historical legacy of the imagery speaks across generations. For example, the 'MFC' representing the Melbourne Football Club was first used in 1859, while baseball's Cincinnati 'red stockings' appeared as early as 1869.

Whether a logo or a symbol expresses a brand's personality, or has the personality instilled in it through association-infused marketing communication, remains a complex and sometimes controversial question. Abstract designs (such as Ferrari's prancing horse) may be recognisable because of their distinctive nature, but often require significant marketing communication efforts to explain or instil a meaning to sport consumers. More natural or direct designs, such as Major League Baseball's swinging batter silhouette, can be immediately and intuitively understood.

Irrespective of the amount of effort required to instil the meaning attached to logos and symbols, associations come through a process of learning. Sport consumers – whether they purchase a brand or not – come to associate logos or symbols with certain brands, and then subsequently to associate certain concepts with those logos, which may have valuable marketing connotations. The learning process is powerful to marketers as it provides a way of helping consumers make the necessary connections automatic and seamless.

A symbol or logo can, to paraphrase an old cliché, be worth a thousand words, not to mention a billion dollars. As an example, consider the Olympic rings, the brand logo of the Olympic Games and usually received worldwide as a recognised symbol of achievement. The powerful associations that accompany the rings are not overlooked by the multinational companies that pay tens of millions of dollars to use the symbolism in their advertising, or indeed by the major cities around the world who fight long and expensive campaigns to win the right to host the Olympic Games.

Successful logos are easily recognised, convey consistent messages to target audiences, and evoke positive feelings.[23] Their embedded meanings and associations hold the power to change consumer perceptions of a logo's parent brand, and therefore its custodian sport enterprise. Great logos also tend to be versatile, culturally transferrable, easily updated, relevant, and appropriate in a range of product categories.[24] Furthermore, in the world of branding, familiarity breeds favourability, proving that smart branding starts with awareness, and then moves on to repetition.

Brand names and URLs

Brand names and their associated website address (URL) comprise an increasingly significant component of a brand. They can express the key benefit of a product and are usually prominently displayed in various forms of marketing, including having names or abbreviations of them (e.g., MUFC for Manchester United Football Club) as hashtags for easy searchability on social media platforms. The selection of a suitable brand name and associated web address for a product is critical as they play a decisive role in brand awareness by distinguishing a brand from competitors, describing a brand and its attributes or benefits, achieving compatibility with a brand's desired image and with its product design or packaging, and enhancing memorability.[25]

For sporting brands, the name is often inherent in a geographical location, although a flourish by allowing a team to add a memorable descriptor or a nickname is typical, with the term forming a powerful branding platform. Los Angeles's world-famous entertainment market is dominated by the 'Lakers,' a name that originated in 1948 when the team was playing in Minneapolis, in the state of Minnesota, famous for its lakes. When the team moved to Los Angeles in 1960, they took the name with them, building a level of recognition among basketball fans around the world that remains omnipresent. Given the relative uniqueness of the name, it can also be more easily protected legally, lending the term even greater marketing clout due to its exclusivity. When the South Melbourne Soccer Club, a powerhouse of the National Soccer League in Australia, was dissuaded from continuing to use the ethnic term 'Hellas' as its nickname in the 1990s, the club turned to the term Lakers in search of a broader market given the team literally played next to Melbourne's famous Albert Park Lake. That decision proved short-lived, with calls for change by many fans (and apparently the Los Angeles Lakers themselves, despite their distance and different sport).

Characters and spokespeople

Brand characters and spokespeople can be woven into marketing campaigns, most commonly through the advertising component. They can arrive in animated forms or represent celebrity or typical-person endorsers. Characters and spokespeople provide a number of benefits, the most evident of which is their dual ability to first attract attention to the brand, and then to humanise it.[26] Character representatives often provide symbols of the entire brand in their own sense. For example, McDonald's set the benchmark in using the 'Ronald McDonald' clown character in promotional campaigns, advertisements, point-of-sale material, and other marketing collateral (such as tray liners, playground equipment, and children's toys), as a prominent representation of their family, fun focus. Similarly, in the lead up to the controversial 1980 Moscow Olympic Games, the cute, perky-eared bear, Misha, appeared in much of the Games' imagery, from the commercial marketing to the political propaganda.

Sporting teams are somewhat unique in that their rich history and tapestry frequently reveals spokespeople who can speak with authority because their own personal brand is so entwined with that of the sporting organisation. Sir Alex Ferguson's every utterance is dissected carefully by fans of Manchester United long after he left the managerial role, while the media often turns to past players, coaches, and associates of leading teams to provide commentary. For many sporting clubs, this means that spokespeople are far and wide, although they are not always 'officially' part of the marketing message.

Slogans and jingles

Sometimes brands use alliterations or short statements in the form of slogans to simultaneously solicit attention, and to help stick in the memory. A slogan can be defined as a short phrase focusing on a description about the brand's character, a comment about a unique product feature, an expectation about the experience of its consumption, or a reminder about another aspect of a product's (or its parent brand's) nature and delivery, such as price, availability, or service. Famous example are, of course, Nike's 'Just Do It,' which is emblematic of the brand's spirit of action, and Disneyland's 'The Happiest Place on Earth,' which is a bold claim to its status as a globally recognised location of joy for young and old.

A slogan may make an official brand promise, characterise a philosophy, encapsulate a company's intentions to its target audience, or link to a brand's ethos as a result of successful marketing campaigns. They can even extend into musical representations, or jingles, of a brand's attributes or benefits, usually with the aim of prompting memorability. Slogans can appear in advertising and promotional campaigns, including as hashtags on social media, but they also appear as part of a product's packaging, or even be emblazoned on the product itself, which, of course, is commonplace for sporting equipment. For example, cricket equipment manufacturer GM displays the slogan 'England's Best' on their bats, using two words to make an emphatic case for their product quality.

Slogans and jingles can play a number of roles in helping to build brand equity. They can assist in creating recall by linking a brand back to its category by using a direct reference to the brand and category relationship, or by creating a sense of emotion attached to the brand. Who wouldn't want to play at Manchester United's 'Theatre of Dreams' irrespective of whether you followed the team or not? In addition, slogans give marketers a 'hook' as a means of identifying the positioning of a brand relative to competitors. FC Barcelona proudly boasts of being 'Més que un club' (more than a club), while the Ultimate Fighting Championship (UFC) launched itself in the early 1990s with the tagline, 'There are no rules,' to suggest their rugged positioning in the marketplace. Having become so important, brand owners typically seek to legally protect their slogans by applying to have them registered as trademarks.

Packaging and colour

Packaging and colour can act as distinct elements but are often inter-related given that they play a strong role in identifying a brand and also in conveying persuasive and descriptive information. Packaging builds brand equity as it is directly implicated in the purchase or usage of products, particularly fast-moving consumer goods such as energy drinks and sporting supplements. A package may be the last piece of marketing collateral that a sport consumer sees before purchasing a product, and may be causally related to a consumer's decision to use the product itself. Accordingly, packaging proves decisive in brand identification and thus in the success of a product.

Colour constitutes one of seven key packaging features (the others being typography, logo, material, shape, label, and size).[27] Association between a brand and a colour or colour scheme commands power because it ensures that consumers can readily identify a brand in a competitive marketplace, and/or when they make decisions based on past brand experience or knowledge. In this respect, colour delivers a strong visual cue in the identification process that can be critical to a consumer's decision-making.[28] The effect can also be emotive rather than just as a cue, mainly through the stimulus to house emotive signals as symbolic metaphors formed through associative learning.[29] As a result, the mere use of a specific colour can provide a cue for consumer recognition and for attaching meaningful associations. By virtue of its emotive connotations, colour mobilises a salient sport branding attribute, particularly where a short decision timeframe exists.

As we have previously discussed, colour is also a powerful symbol for sport consumers who internalise this visual signal as a representation of their fandom. They paint their faces in club colours, they proudly decorate their homes and cars in club colours, and will even speak of (metaphorically) bleeding in the club palette should it come to that. The choice of colour in sport is often historically significant, such as the yellow leader's jersey in the Tour de France, but in more modern times has been matched by a marketing sophistication geared towards maximising revenue from ancillary sales such as merchandise. As a result, some sport teams are willing to adopt 'retro' colours of years past or tie their colour choices for particular matches into a sponsor linkage as a revenue-generating idea.

Creative style

In communicating with their target audiences, brands often develop a style or creative approach that, over time and with repetition, becomes strongly aligned to the brand. For example, Apple represents a creative style that prioritises design and exploration above pure computing power or tech-speak. This creative style is by its very nature difficult to define, but typically represents a framework for communication that involves a unique structure, sequence, tone, or personality. Unlike the previously mentioned elements, creative style is difficult to pin down, and therefore tends to be limited both in use and in importance as a brand element. However, by definition, the creative style used to convey a message is present at the nexus of communication between consumer and brand. As such, while not being part of the actual product, it can become part of a brand's identity, like in the way we might expect a certain aggressiveness in marketing and branding communications from Nike. Similarly, the Oakland Raiders of the NFL have become famous for their bold marketing that mimics the super-charged competitiveness of the team. The National Basketball Association (NBA) is another global example, portraying its brand as one of relentless action that is amplified by individual superstars who compete against one another. The NBA's creative style is unashamedly 'young' and 'fresh,' featuring numerous social media elements, high-energy fast-cut action, and an emphasis on individual stars who are encouraged to interact with fans in a range of modes.

Conclusion – concept to creation

To recap, at its most basic level, a sport brand is a name, term, symbol, sign, or design, or a combination of these elements, which identifies a product to consumers by differentiating it from the product offerings of competitors. These items in themselves can be viewed as brand elements or brand components, which serve to provide a distinction between brands.[30] A brand derives its relevance from the relationship between these elements and the way that consumers conceptualise the elements in their minds.

The development of strong sport brands is both desirable and valuable. Strong brands allow sport consumers to readily distinguish the products of a sport enterprise and to associate positive and/or desirable elements with it. The resulting value is commonly referred to as brand equity, which, in turn, allows a sport organisation to increase sales and profits, increase its valuation as an ongoing entity, and plan its marketing operations with a degree of certainty and continuity. Brand equity results from branding activities that are clear, consistent, and strategically coordinated, representing the brand via brand elements, which may include a visual style, logo, executional emphasis, character, or colour, and then links these to tangible and intangible associations, meanings, and benefits of value to customers.

Notes

1 Keller, K.L. (2003). *Strategic Brand Management*. Upper Saddle River, NJ: Pearson at page 4.
2 Keller, K.L. (2003). *Strategic Brand Management*. Upper Saddle River, NJ: Pearson.
3 Aaker, D.A. (2002). *Building Strong Brands*. London: Simon & Schuster at page 10.
4 Kapferer, J.N. (2008). *The New Strategic Brand Management*. London: Kogan Page at page 2.
5 Keller, K.L. (2003). *Strategic Brand Management*. Upper Saddle River, NJ: Pearson.
6 Fournier, S. (1998). Consumers and their brands: Developing relationship theory in consumer research. *Journal of Consumer Research, 24*(4), 343–374.
7 Roberts, K. (2004). *Lovemarks: The Future Beyond Brands*. New York: Power House Books.
8 Keller, K.L. (2003). *Strategic Brand Management*. Upper Saddle River, NJ: Pearson.
9 Aaker, D.A. (1996). *Building Strong Brands*. New York: Free Press.
10 Aaker, D.A. (1991). *Managing Brand Equity: Capitalizing on the Value of a Brand Name*. New York: Free Press.
11 Rossiter, J.R., & Bellman, S. (2005). *Marketing Communications: Theory and Applications*. Frenchs Forest, NSW: Pearson.
12 Keller, K.L. (2003). *Strategic Brand Management*. Upper Saddle River, NJ: Pearson at page 61.
13 Aaker, D.A. (1996). *Building Strong Brands*. New York: Free Press at pages 7–8
14 McWilliams J.D. (2016). *Coca-Cola no. 3 on most valuable brands ranking*. Retrieved from https://www.coca-colacompany.com/stories/coca-cola-no-3-on-most-valuable-brands-ranking.
15 Kotler, P., & Keller, K.L. (2006). *Marketing Management*. Upper Saddle River, NJ: Pearson.

16 Sandritter, M. (2016). *The Broncos lose every Super Bowl in orange, so they are wearing white in Super Bowl 50.* Retrieved from https://www.sbnation.com/lookit/2016/1/25/10830582/denver-broncos-super-bowl-50-white-jerseys-panthers.

17 Sutherland, M. (1993). *Advertising and the Mind of the Consumer.* St. Leonards, NSW: Allen & Unwin.

18 Smith. A.C.T. (2008). *Introduction to Sport Marketing.* Burlington, MA: Butterworth-Heinemann.

19 Wann, D.L. (1995). Preliminary validation of the sport fan motivation scale. *Journal of Sport and Social Issues, 19*(4), 377–396.

20 O'Sullivan, G. (2010). The relationship between hope, eustress, self-efficacy, and life satisfaction among undergraduates. *Social Indicators Research, 101*(1), 155–172.

21 International Paralympic Committee (2017). *Brand book.* Retrieved from https://www.paralympic.org/sites/default/files/document/170801095817878_2017_07%2BIPC%2BBrand%2BBook.pdf.

22 Keller, K.L. (2003). *Strategic Brand Management.* Upper Saddle River, NJ: Pearson.

23 Henderson, P.W., & Cote, J.A. (1998). Guidelines for selecting or modifying logos. *Journal of Marketing, 62*(2), 14–30.

24 Keller, K.L. (2003). *Strategic Brand Management.* Upper Saddle River, NJ: Pearson.

25 Shimp T. (2007). *Advertising, Promotion and Other Aspects of Integrated Marketing Communication.* Mason, OH: Cengage.

26 Keller, K.L. (2003). *Strategic Brand Management.* Upper Saddle River, NJ: Pearson.

27 Pickton, D., & Broderick A. (2001). *Integrated Marketing Communications.* Harlow: Pearson.

28 Hine. T. (1995). *The Total Package.* Boston, MA: Little Brown and Co.

29 Grossman, R.P., & Wisenblit, J.Z. (1999). What we know about consumers' color choices. *Journal of Marketing Practice: Applied Marketing Science, 5*(3), 78–88.

30 Keller, K.L. (2003). *Strategic Brand Management.* Upper Saddle River, NJ: Pearson.

3 Mobilising sport brands

Introduction – beginning with sport consumer behaviour

In the previous two sections we examined sport branding from a rudimentary perspective, chiefly through a prism of functional elements that convey meaning via strategically positioned symbols and signals. In this section, we will deepen our conceptualisation of sport branding by considering the more complex relationship between branding elements and sport consumers.

The International Olympic Committee (IOC) has one of the most powerful sporting brands in the world. Many children around the world dream of one day appearing in the Olympic Games, representing their country and winning the cherished gold medal emblematic of rarefied elite sporting success. Some who achieve Olympic team selection will even celebrate by having the famous five 'Olympic rings' tattooed on their body.[1] Despite its pre-eminence, there is no lull in the IOC's branding drive. The IOC recognises that branding demands a continual process of adjustment to ensure a fit with ever diverse target audiences. As a result, the IOC has, in recent years, attempted to better understand and respond to the behaviour of sport consumers by changing its product offering through the provision of new Olympic sports that are thought to better represent contemporary tastes.[2]

Olympic competitions have traditionally been conservative and staid, a reflection of the event's historical legacy. However, the Games' greatest strength also makes for a severe weakness, necessitating a reliance on heritage for marketing success. Eager to make the brand appear progressive and appealing to a youthful audience, the IOC has enacted constant change in order to maintain its position as a globally unifying spectacle. The IOC has tended to be most fluid when dealing with the winter version of its event, perhaps demonstrating that this format is most conducive to innovation, including snowboarding 'big air' and snowboard 'cross' competitions that present a form of extreme sports built on huge jumps and flashy tricks.

The Summer Olympics is not immune from change, with the Tokyo 2020 games featuring five new sports along with new events within existing sports, including 3-on-3 basketball, a game that emerged on the streets of major cities in the United States.[3] In making these changes, and planning more, the IOC appears cognisant that their brand will be viewed as 'moving with the times' in matching consumer desire for action, while facilitating a product that will be appealing to their biggest benefactors, the television broadcasters which pay billions of US dollars for the rights to be associated with the potent Olympic brand.

Prior to responding to perceptions of consumer desire or behaviour, a sport brand, from the might of the IOC to a smaller label selling sport clothing, must first seek to understand the type of consumer who purchases, or is likely to purchase, the sporting goods or services offered for sale. For example, Lululemon Athletica is a successful brand in the active sportswear market that is designed to appeal to participants who can appreciate both the athletic function of the product and the broader fashion appeal of activewear. The company, which originally began making apparel for yoga enthusiasts, has cleverly interpreted the way activewear clothing has become part of modern fashion culture. The result has led to an unprecedented global expansion based upon the brand's resonant juxtaposition of social acceptance and healthy pursuits.

For sporting brands to succeed over the longer term, they must become particularly adept at understanding the behaviour of consumers, including how their feelings and motivations might change over time. Successful sporting enterprises also must adjust their branding strategies in response to changing consumer perceptions. For example, fast food companies like McDonald's have reacted to consumer preferences for more wholesome choices by introducing a range of healthier and fresher menu items as well as a more aggressive sponsorship strategy around sport and physical activity. In looking to the future, sport brands must also hold on to existing fans who may be drawn to traditional elements of the brand, just as McDonald's would never discard its 'Big Mac,' despite the introduction of newer product choices.

Balancing tradition with innovation is often challenging in sport but can be met by governing bodies through the creation of new brands that allow different audiences to remain connected to product offerings that match their needs, without diluting the appeal of traditional elements. The sport of cricket, once chided for being ultra-conservative, is now an exemplar of progression, featuring a range of branded products, including T20 Cricket, a fast-paced form of the game that appeals to young, contemporary audiences. Motorsport has embraced Formula E, an electric-powered open-wheel racing series, while, as noted earlier, sports such as basketball have embraced their street culture by promoting a 3-on-3 version of the game for the Olympics.

In order to understand consumer behaviour and make the right branding responses, sport brands typically undertake market research, aiming to gather key information about the needs, wants, and preferences of their customers and fans. Market research can vary from specific qualitative or quantitative studies, through to the general analysis of trends or consumption patterns. Even when a sport brand does not undertake its own unique and directed research, it will nevertheless monitor the actions of competitors in order to frame its positioning strategy within a market context. Building on the earlier example, a competitor to McDonald's may not have done any specific research about consumers' reactions to offering healthier menu items, but would have been faced with a strategic decision to consider such a move once becoming aware of McDonald's new initiative.

To continue the illustration using an apparel example, a brand such as adidas must find ways to deliver both function and fashion requirements through its product ranges. Dealing with such tensions requires constant monitoring and attention, which means staying abreast of advancements in material technologies (via research and development activities), while at the same time remaining in-tune with fashion trends, market fads, and fickle consumer penchants. Additionally, there is a need to monitor a vast array of competitors, all of whom may be on to the next 'big thing.' Thus, the process of sport branding for a power brand such as adidas swings between prosaic product demands, competitor actions, and compelling fashion desires, the intersection of which is expressed through a brand's elements and its visual connection with consumers.

The visual connection embodies the brand identity that sport consumers and fans display as part of their own personal characters. By inference, a brand's identity is inextricably connected to consumers' self-perceptions as individuals and what attributes they want to display to friends, family, colleagues, and the broader public. For example, when we pull on a pair of adidas shoes, eat a burger at McDonald's, or cheer loudly for a Ferrari racing driver, we are sending a message to those around us, whether we want to or not. Brands are supremely conscious of how consumers use their brands as personal projections, and work hard to ensure that their brand image represents something that a consumer in their target audience would want to be connected to. All of us as consumers are faced with enormous challenges in navigating the efforts of brands to mobilise their behaviour into a form of consumption.

Branding and choice

Unlike a sporting enterprise that may be dealing with the development and promotion of just one overarching brand and a handful of products, sport consumers juggle relationships with thousands of brands, most of which may be of little interest. In most cases, sport consumers need to be exposed to basic, repetitive, single-issue messages over a sustained period for a sport brand to secure some traction in their memories. Keep in mind that just because sport fans are often seen to have fanatical behaviours to one or a small number of teams or sports, this doesn't necessarily transfer to all their entertainment or consumption experiences. A passion for one football team might also coexist with casual interests that a consumer has in a range of other sports – from archery to volleyball – that do not necessarily translate into high levels of interest despite their entertainment value. Most people can relate to a lower level of involvement, particularly with sports such as figure skating that may capture attention once every four years when on prime-time television, before fading from mainstream appeal.

Consumers tend not to know much about many of the brands they interact with, preferring by necessity to only remember the most pertinent information. For a sport brand to maximise its chance of seeding some interest in a consumer's mind amidst all the clutter of competition and marketing noise, it needs to appreciate the character of choice and the decision-making process that exists. Sport invariably exists as an entertainment product, so competition is fierce, dynamic, and relentless, especially as the digital age heralds new experiences that go well beyond merely being a spectator.

Consumers typically undergo a five-stage hierarchical process when considering the purchase or usage of a product.[4] These steps were introduced briefly earlier in the book in their generic marketing form and are explored in detail specifically from a sporting perspective.

Recognition of a problem – this is the point where a sport consumer's actual state differs significantly enough from their desired state that they commit to taking some action to resolve the discrepancy. Recognition of a problem can happen naturally (e.g., needing a pair of football boots to participate in a match), or be brought on by communication from a brand (e.g., seeing a billboard announcing a new style of shoe and then feeling a desire to obtain it). From a branding viewpoint, sport managers must make an important decision at this foundational stage of the hierarchical process, which is whether to invest funds in stimulating this problem – a use of resources that may be considerable and lead consumers to adopting rival brands – or allow this problem to rise to a salient level for consumers naturally, thus letting the investment in building and communicating brand elements to be diverted to the following areas.

Search for information – after recognising a problem (whether self-initiated or not), a sport consumer will search for information concerning a range of possible solutions. It might take the form of a simple mental search like, for example, a quick scan of memory to see what brands can be recalled, or might involve a more systematic search, such as looking at websites, visiting stores, considering published reviews, talking to sales people, and seeking advice from peers. The critical strategic decision here for brands lies in ensuring that their brand elements are available in all the places a consumer is likely to search: from internal, where building brand recall by embedding characteristics in short-term memory will be helpful, right through to ensuring brand elements are visible from web browser searching, location visits, or when consumers seek recommendations from friends. The ubiquity of sport makes it particularly appealing to brands seeking to be noticed. For example, sponsorship often aims to ensure that consumers notice brands in their search process. In a world where advertising is easily bypassed, marketers have invariably noticed that live sport attracts not only large audiences, but also captive ones.[5]

Evaluation of alternatives – for simple decisions, a consumer will weigh up options automatically at the same time as they conduct their search, but often the evaluation occurs at a later point when a consumer believes that they have sufficient information to either narrow the decision or make a selection. At the evaluation stage, a consumer will use a range of criteria based upon their personal circumstances and requirements in order to mentally rank the possible choices. The criteria might change depending upon the situation. For example, an evaluation of a suitable sporting event to attend would be different if a minor were involved compared to a group of adults. That is, appropriate content will take on a greater priority, where ultimate fighting will be viewed differently to, say, ice-skating. As with the previous searching stage, the process of evaluation can transpire swiftly, almost instantaneously, or involve a complex trade-off where a consumer grapples with choices that all will yield some benefits, but none will deliver everything sought. For sport branding managers, it may be necessary at this point to carefully evaluate what a brand offering has that other rivals do not. Some sports will allow children to attend for free if accompanied by an adult, while others might highlight a once-in-a-lifetime opportunity to see a star in action, thus elevating the evaluation to one highlighting scarcity. The Australian Football League (AFL) has long tried to attract fans to its sport by highlighting its combination of a mixture of skills from other popular sports around the world, presenting a 'package' of excitement that can appeal across a broad range of tastes and demographics.

Purchase decision – assuming that all has gone well thus far (a consumer may stop at any point if dissatisfied with the process or because of a re-evaluation of the circumstances), the next stage involves making a selection. Selection involves several levels where choices can be made, including the product, the brand, and the store (site or channel of sales). Again, like the previous stages, the purchase decision can move quickly (e.g., in the case of impulse purchases), or take considerable time as consumers continue to search and evaluate before committing to a purchase (e.g., the acquisition of a major new piece of sporting equipment). For sport branding managers, the purchase decision is a critical one as it is directly linked to tangible sales and profits. Some brands may leverage the opportunity for consumer decision-making at this point by heavily applying their resources to point-of-sale branding that attracts attention and can motivate a sale. For example, a smaller golf club manufacturer which specialises in high-quality clubs might not have the marketing budget of major rivals such as Ping, Titleist, or TaylorMade, preferring to set up displays in golf stores in the hope that the efforts of their rivals to bring consumers into the store will give them a chance to make a sale, offering an alternative range just as the consumer is making a purchase decision.

Usage and post-purchase behaviour – the consumer decision-making process does not end with a purchase. A consumer's usage of the product and subsequent feelings about it will linger in his or her memory and directly affect the possibility of re-purchase. Naturally, when a consumer is satisfied with a product, the chances of a future re-purchase increases, although it is always possible that some consumers may decide to never buy it again because they are variety seekers (e.g., in choosing a sport tourism destination), or simply because their purchase represents a one-off activity, like attending an Olympic event in their home city. In the case of products that offer solutions to everyday problems, a consumer will hastily form strong opinions as to whether their needs have been met, and therefore whether re-purchase seems appealing. This post-purchase behaviour is internalised, allowing a consumer to feed the information back into future situations where they might make purchasing decisions, and, of course, they can also externalise their decision-making by sharing their views with others via word-of-mouth or word-of-mouse. Many golfers, for example, may have been drawn to trying a new driver on the recommendations or reviews that they may encounter in-person or online. For brands, facilitating reviews remains critical, both in generating positive news and in attenuating unfavourable commentaries. Increasingly, post-purchase behaviour is being recorded by consumers offering detailed reviews and opinions, which can range from a simple one line on a forum, right through to professionally designed and edited videos on YouTube. A sport brand must pay attention to this stage of the consumer process, as it represents the point where the loop is closed and will feed back into subsequent behaviour. It is important to remember that given the ephemeral and unpredictable nature of many sporting experiences, brands might well be asking a fan to return and repurchase when their experience has been one of watching their favoured team lose. Motivating consumers in such situations is challenging, with branding forming the long-term associations that smooth out negative outcomes.

Brands and brand elements play a pivotal role during all the stages noted earlier, not just at obvious points such as the search for information. As has been highlighted, they can help to initiate the recognition of a problem, identify possible product offerings, provide information to assist with evaluation in making appropriate decisions, and shape the usage and evaluation of a product made by consumers.

One of the easiest ways to understand the purchasing process and thus identify the branding decisions that coincide with them is to map out the stages noted earlier and then ask the following three corresponding questions. Who is involved at each stage? Where do these consumers make their decisions? And finally, when do these consumers make decisions during each stage? By knowing who, where, and when, a brand can create a roadmap that demonstrates the buying stages relative to which consumers need to be targeted, where they need to be targeted, and when they need to be targeted.

For sporting teams that play a regular season, one of the optimal times to try and move consumers through the buying process is right before matches begin, as at that point a powerful message of anticipation can be displayed. In research that has been conducted on motivations of sport fans in a modern, online context, the concept of passion, camaraderie, hope, and esteem proved pivotal.[6] It is at this point that season tickets, sometimes known as 'memberships' in parts of the world where fans buy in to voting and associated rights of governance, are most prominent and can establish a strong financial flow for clubs that leverage their brands to instil a sense of connection to the fans.

Fans are primed at certain points of the year to make a significant commitment if buying season tickets, and given the communal nature of sporting experiences, such purchases are often moments that end up being communicated more broadly.

For brands, understanding who is involved in a buying decision goes well beyond just targeting the person who will make a payment. Families have long shared their sporting passions, meaning that even the youngest (or oldest) of fans can have a significant say in what sports form part of the broader entertainment experience. Children, despite not having a lot of direct purchasing power themselves, are highly influential. Sporting teams around the world know that young fans are often drawn to the 'star power' of athletes, rather than to the appeal of a broader team or sport.

Branding and choice in sport is far more complicated than it first appears. A brand may have to think about various permutations and combinations of who to target, when to target them, and where to target them. An equally important further question then arises regarding 'how' to target them. We'll come to that shortly, but first let's take another step inside the mind of the sport consumer.

Identification and involvement with brand associations

Fans commonly incorporate support for a sporting team as part of their self-identity. In the process, they merge brand associations with self-perceptions, and how they believe others might view them. Integral to this process is how a consumer identifies with groups in society.

Social identity theory embodies the concept of identification, the notion that people associate themselves with particular groups and form identities based on the associations.[7] The theory explains group-based and individual behaviours by suggesting that individuals employ social categories to define others and locate themselves in the social world.[8] Identification with a team, club, or athlete represents a means of constructing or bolstering the self-concept, and can be motivated by numerous factors including the need to maintain and enhance positive personal and social self-evaluations, the need to belong, tribal connections, and a sense of self-efficacy through vicarious achievement.[9] A critical conclusion predicts that emotional attachment becomes more strongly implicated when an individual constructs a sense of self through identification, in this case with a sporting brand.

Involvement in the consumer behaviour context refers to the personal relevance a consumer feels concerning the product category under consideration, and, by consequence, the purchase decision. In the case of a low-involvement product, the consumer perceives little risk in purchasing the product and may do so automatically, committing little time or mental resources to searching, evaluation, or consideration. Conversely, a high-involvement product will be more important to a consumer due to greater perceived social or financial risk. A high-involvement purchase entails active consideration of a myriad of factors, along with a correspondingly thoughtful evaluation process.

The five behavioural stages discussed earlier directly relate to the intensity of involvement a consumer experiences with the sporting products that have attracted their attention. Since the level of involvement a consumer exhibits with a brand typically reflects the amount of risk (social, financial, or both) in the decision, a low involvement product or decision will likely mean that a consumer will move through the stages rapidly and without the need for lengthy consideration. Here, the consumer purchases on impulse or is comfortable with the product or brand and the satisfaction that it brings. Conversely, high involvement products will involve the expenditure of greater resources in the decision process, leading to more searching, evaluation, consideration, and post-purchase analysis. A high-involvement purchase will likely become less involved as experience increases.

Consumer decisions do not need to be categorically high or low involvement. A continuum operates between these extremes wherein consumers can shift as decision circumstances evolve. For example, whether to attend a local tennis tournament might be a low-involvement decision until a friend or relative happens to be participating, whereupon involvement shifts up substantively.

For many consumers, a relationship with a sporting brand presents a high-involvement decision given the relationship is typically one that is enduring. A fan of the New England Patriots is unlikely to switch allegiance with any ease. That does not necessarily mean that subsequent decisions to interact with the brand become any easier, or become lower in involvement. Unlike typical consumer products, which can, over time, become routine or repetitive, sport's strong social connection both to a fan's identity and to feelings of personal value more broadly, will often resonate strongly, making each and every interaction significant. For sport fans who feel truly attached to a brand, each interaction becomes something of importance.

Moments-of-truth

Given that sport is a service, what is often being 'sold' in the core context of an event represents a unique engagement. While brands that associate themselves with sport might be offering something tangible, such as sportswear, beer, or a piece of merchandise, sport at its heart is a shared, ephemeral, perishable, and heterogeneous moment. These moments combine to form an experience measured against expectations.

The beauty (although some might argue it reflects the ugly complexity) of sport is that its experiential moments are largely unpredictable. In a world of the unknown, a brand can take on a magical aura of invincibility, fallibility, or inspiration that will resonate from its mercurial moments-of-truth.

The moments-of-truth concept stormed into popular use in the 1980s when a Scandinavian airline executive, Jan Carlzon, spoke of the many thousands of uncertain moments passengers face each day, from booking a ticket to disembarking the flight and collecting their luggage.[10] Sporting brands encounter a similar process, as spectators and fans use the cues and interactions of countless moments to judge their experience. Even the most hardened fan might feel some, albeit bittersweet, 'joy' at a loss, knowing that their team fought valiantly, or that the event was enjoyable or memorable. For sporting brands, managing moments-of-truth has become critical, but remains contingent upon their successful mapping. This is a form of blueprinting that takes the ephemeral and tries to build it into something measurable.

The measurement of experiential moments comprises a correlation between expectations and reality, with the interaction either falling above, below, or in line with expectations. Obviously, the greater expectations can be exceeded, the greater the perceived brand happiness that will result. For Leicester City fans, the 2015–2016 English Premier League season was one of surreal joy, as their team, which some expected would finish far closer to the bottom of the table than the top, surprised the world and won the league title. The case reveals how mapping experience moments reflects the life journey of fans, understanding the decisive events that might occur along the way, and how the relationship with a brand will develop. Sporting brands tend not to be fleeting. Most will play the long game – a part of a broader identity and not just a transaction or a commodity. As a consequence, sport branding takes on a special meaning where brands are employed to nurture and connect with other associated brands.

Masterbrands and an integrated communications approach

We have already foreshadowed the importance of integrated marketing communications as the prevailing paradigm in the advertising and promotion industry. Further, its approach permeates through branding as well given that every aspect of marketing, from product to pricing, is mediated through a brand's messaging. Integrated marketing communications (IMC) involves the systematic combination of marketing activities to provide clarity, consistency, and maximum impact of brand communications to a sport enterprise's target audience.[11] IMC might be seen as analogous to a symphony orchestra, where all the elements are playing in perfect synchronicity, thus creating a perfect summation of individual parts in a clear, resonant, and cohesive manner. That same analogy can carry through to the orchestra where each member plays their own tune. Technically it is music, but the odd combinations will cut through any harmony, rendering the resultant 'noise' to be musical, but misaligned and meaningless. For sporting brands and their many stakeholders, playing synchronistically can often prove harder than it first appears.

Consumers' and fans' perceptions of a sporting enterprise and its various brands arrive as a synthesis of a diverse set of consumer experiences beyond just moments-of-truth, including, for example, packaging, price, the store or channel through which the product is acquired, advertising, and sales promotion. IMC aims to ensure that all of these mechanisms provide a consistent and positive experiential theme for the consumer. It goes well beyond the use of a common slogan, packaging, or colour. Rather, IMC strives to create the maximum possible synergy between all the various elements making up consumer contact points, whether a specific advertisement, a delivery van, or a ticketed entrance.

An example of an IMC approach can be seen with a sport brand such as Wimbledon, the famed tennis championship, that seeks to communicate its unique English heritage through its advertising, the 'look and feel' of its venue (its livery and internal fit-out like seat covers and colour schemes), the uniforms of staff, the style of interaction delivered, and the types of supplemental services that it supports and from which it receives sponsorship. Consistency across the full range of contact points allows sport consumers to understand a brand, what its offerings comprise, and its explicit and implicit promises. Done well, full integration leaves the sport consumer with no ambiguity about what the brand stands for, and subsequently enhances the brand's ability to engender confidence and loyalty. IMC also reduces overall marketing costs (through both efficiency and synergy of communications effort), increases sales, and augments brand equity through superior brand awareness and positive brand attitude.

Brands move towards integrated communication by ensuring that their product offerings link, wherever possible, to common brand elements. For example, elements may include colour (e.g., the use of an elegant silver by Mercedes-Benz in much of their marketing communications); a slogan (e.g., Mercedes-Benz' 'the best or nothing'); a consistent advertising style (e.g., Mercedes-Benz generally uses high quality print and electronic advertising that matches the prestige position of their brand); the types of events with which the brand is associated (e.g., Mercedes-Benz is prominently involved in leading motor-racing events, sponsoring fashion festivals and is even the naming sponsor of the stadium in Atlanta that hosted the 2019 Super Bowl); and the message transferred (e.g., Mercedes-Benz is a mixture of aspirational luxury and cutting-edge technology).

The same consistency can be applied to a brand such as Wimbledon. Green and purple backdrops display a royal and resplendent contrast to the all-white clothing of players, the catering features high-end food, the associated sponsors reflect precision and luxury, and ticketing is carefully controlled to create a sense of scarcity and exclusivity. As an integrated summation, Wimbledon prides itself on being the ultimate tennis tournament, trading on its no-nonsense tradition to exude authenticity, authority, and ambition to both participants and fans. It's no surprise that young tennis players aspire to ultimately win at Wimbledon, assured that aligning their personal brand to that of the storied tennis tournament that has been played since 1877 is the epitome of achievement.

The game of golf also has an equally storied and textured brand. For example, The Masters tournament in the United States is the only one of the four 'Majors' in golf to be played at the same course each year, that is, Augusta National in the state of Georgia. While a great deal can be said about The Masters, which has run since 1934, the central branding approach has always centred on an understated confidence that the tournament needs little branding beyond its name and reputation.

Augusta National takes immense pride in providing a highly exclusive members-only club that trades on privacy and tradition. The winner of The Masters traditionally receives a 'green jacket,' a symbol of membership to the club. While all golf events require significant sponsorship to ensure financial survival, The Masters keeps its business relationships to a necessary minimum, strictly policing the signage that can be used and how the event can be referred to. In fact, the event limits anything that may be seen as intruding on the purity of the spectacle. While most sporting events clamour for media attention and salivate at the prospect of attracting bigger numbers through media and sponsorship, The Masters appears largely unfazed, adopting an approach that marketing is not forced if the brand is supremely appealing. Of course, such an approach is a form of marketing in itself, and it surely works. While some may claim that the British Open remains the golf tournament of elite aspiration, many others would argue that The Masters now presents the premiere tournament in the world, and perhaps the leader on the 'bucket list' of fans across the globe seeking the ultimate sporting experience. As a brand, 'The Masters' stands among the elite of the sporting mountain top, having earned its reputation not by marketing gimmickry, but through a purist passion to steer clear of excess; branding without trying to brand – a salient lesson in a world where consumers can be cynical and sceptical of marketing efforts and find what they might perceive as pure experiences most attractive. In the context of branding, it therefore pays to remember that sometimes less is more. In effect, giving consumers the right pieces to the branding puzzle and letting them sort it out for themselves can be a stronger outcome than one enforcing branding through commercialism or short-term messages.

One common method for instilling a brand-wide and carefully controlled IMC approach that will resist excesses, involves the introduction of a 'masterbrand.' From a strategic viewpoint, a masterbrand specifies a considered, carefully structured visual style that explicitly details the look, characteristics, and identity of products, signage, displays, uniforms, letterhead, and so forth, across the sport enterprise and product range. The masterbrand is typically expressed and specified via a technical document that a brand and its agents employ as a strict guide to ensure compliance and coherence. The International Paralympic Committee, for example, mentioned in the previous chapter, has a 'Brand Book' online, which details precisely how its branding should appear, including precise colour applications, photo choices, and tone of voice.[12]

A masterbrand strategy reflects the assumption that consumer brand associations – and hence brand equity – are created and built over time and with considerable persistence, investment, and planning. Constructing strong mental associations between the brand and consumers comes through the synergistic effects of orchestrated communications at a variety of targeted audience contact points. For example, these could include knocking on household doors to present the features and benefits of a product in person, sponsoring an event in the hope that such an association might convey positive attributes to consumers, buying advertising time on a commercial television network to broadcast a specific message to a large audience, setting up a social media site to encourage interaction between consumers, constructing point-of-purchase displays in stores to attract attention, and the use of media stories about a brand for publicity. Irrespective of the methods a brand could use, the key factor remains that the consumer must process the communicated information and form some meaning as a result of their exposure to it, in-so-doing putting together a mental picture of puzzle pieces.

Consider, for example, how a sport consumer might view herself as a regular consumer of Under Armour in that wherever possible she prefers to purchase Under Armour sporting gear. Under Armour communicates with her directly (via email, direct mail, SMS, etc.), advertises to her (via television, billboards, website, etc.), and also interacts with her indirectly (social media, in-store representatives, etc.). All of these communication channels provide this sport consumer with information about Under Armour products that she will subsequently weigh up, aggregate, and use to form an understanding of the brand, both in its own right and also in how it compares to competitors and their products.

Integrated approaches, although well understood by sport managers, are often poorly grasped by consumers who view masterbranding as officious, or, in the case of government-funded sporting associations, a waste of resources that could be better used elsewhere. In 2019, the AFL was reported to be reconsidering a redesign of its logo, which had been in place for 20 years at the time.[13] The potential change was reported by the media and met with a measure of negative public reaction. Some fans felt that spending hundreds of thousands of dollars on what appeared to be a cosmetic change would take money away from junior or regional development of the sport. Inflamed by media commentators arguing that a child could design a logo, many fans misunderstood the broader branding process that was in play. For a professional organisation such as the AFL, a change in logo was essentially a reconsideration of their entire masterbrand, which had in recent years grown to include a professional women's league as well as a modified contemporary version of the game called AFLX. With a multimillion dollar merchandising business, and keen to display their 'brand' across the competitive entertainment landscape that existed – including new forms of media – a brand review would be a standard requirement for any organisation in this situation. While a non-sport brand could and would undertake such an action with little or no scrutiny, a sport brand tends to be at the mercy of constant commentary, making a routine branding review a point of conjecture and argument that involves considerable effort to navigate through.

Consumer reaction in these situations stems from their belief, true at least in part, that the managers of many sports do not own the sport but are merely custodians from one generation to the next. Sport consumers therefore tend to view anything that serves to tinker with 'their' sport as something that demands justification. Sport brands should therefore involve their consumers in some branding decisions, allowing them to consider the need for changes to a brand, rather than seeking to impose it upon them.

Brand managers must remain conscious that sport consumers will integrate all the various forms of communication to which they are exposed and use this summation to construct attitudes about their brand, likely leading to an increased or decreased intention to purchase. Keeping communications as simple as possible via a master-brand provides a seamless set of boundaries and guidelines. It should be noted that all instances of contact between a brand and a consumer contribute to the meaning the latter will establish, irrespective of whether it has been planned or not.

Positioning sport brands

As brands are expressed through a set of mental associations, they constitute a range of emotional (feeling) and cognitive (thinking) elements that operate within the minds of consumers. In the case of some brands, it is even possible to demonstrate that this set of associations pivots upon just a few key brand identity elements. It could be argued, for instance, that Nike's renowned 'swoosh' logo comprises a significant brand element, even though the brand experience related to the purchase of some Nike gear involves far more than just the iconic logo. Similarly, Gatorade comprises more than its famous bottle shape, with the container's association with its branded contents having become automatic for millions of sports drink consumers. Marketers strive to connect their brands with identifiable elements as a kind of short-cut to market recognition; it ensures that their brand can be readily recalled. Once an element-awareness has been established, positive and more complex associations can be overlaid upon those elements, which, in turn, transfer over to the brand.

As we introduced earlier in this book, positioning reflects the decisive ways in which sport enterprises aim to locate brand associations in consumers' memories relative to competitors. Through positioning, the custodians of a brand attempt to build a mental niche in relation to competitors by associating unique and distinctive positive elements with a brand. For example, consider how the National Football League's Pittsburgh Steelers has positioned itself as a no-nonsense working-class team compared to the more sophisticated, 'big town' New York Giants or the 'flashy' Dallas Cowboys.

Positioning has become even more important as the volume of advertising has proliferated. When associations work effectively, positioning crashes through the advertising noise, securing a worn groove in the way consumers think, as a result propelling their repeat purchasing. As we have pointed out, a positioning niche may be expressed through a wide range of factors as long as their messages are integrated and complementary. Examples that we have already raised include brand name, slogan, imagery, portrayal of competitors, and colour. Consider a brand such as Ferrari, an exclusive automobile manufacturer that positions itself as reflecting 'Italian style' by assuring consumers of its 'authenticity,' given that Italy is historically viewed as one of the leading exponents of spectacular sports cars. The brand communicates and reinforces its positioning through a prominent connection to elite forms of motor racing, its famous red colour, imagery in advertising that resonates with aspiration, and depictions of the brand's meticulous dedication to continually redefining motoring performance. The same positioning practices occur with other sporting brands too, like surf wear manufacturers Rip Curl, which positions using associations with the laconic Australian surfing town of Torquay, and boxing 'brand' Floyd 'Money' Mayweather, who has elevated his status consistently by associating himself with immense financial deals.

In the sport of boxing, there no better example of an athlete's positioning than the late Muhammad Ali. Born in Louisville, Kentucky, in 1942, as Cassius Clay, Ali rose to international prominence in a surprise defeat of Sonny Liston in 1964 that earned him the honour of being the Heavyweight Champion of the World, a title at the time that was the pinnacle of sporting success. An Olympic gold medallist in 1960, Ali converted to Islam in 1961, adopting his new name, and building a reputation as an athlete who was not afraid to proclaim his talents. In a world where at the time few sportspeople actively engaged with the media, let alone did so in such a bold and brash way, Ali was a phenomenon, speaking poetically and declaring himself 'The Greatest.' It was a title he never shed, even when defeats started to punctuate the end of his career. Ali's greatest strength out of the ring was his ability to attract people's attention, whether they agreed with him or not. His charismatic personality charmed the media, and his role as political icon grew throughout the 60s as he used his global standing – his brand – to push for social causes including racial equality. Ali made international headlines by refusing to be drafted into the US military to serve in the Vietnam War, leading to the revocation of his boxing licence. Ali's brand endured, however, and he is forever associated with some of the greatest moments in sport history.

Arguably the most recognisable sporting athlete brand of the twentieth century, Ali proclaimed a position for himself as the ultimate boxer, the greatest of all time, and fed the perception with a series of heralded bouts that featured elaborate build-ups, enormous global reach for the time, and a sense of theatre that captured the world's imagination. His major bouts, including 'The Rumble in the Jungle' and the 'Thrilla in Manila,' were ground-breaking in their use of showmanship, sponsors, and sport entertainment. Using words, the power of which he understood better than any other athlete at the time, made Ali a household name. However, it is not just saying things, or proclaiming yourself as the best, that can shape a brand. Many other elements are available to sporting brands, particularly as the crowded marketplace makes standing out harder than ever.

For sporting teams, the athletes they choose can say something about their brand's position, with teams such as Real Madrid FC famous for recruiting the world's leading footballing talent, embracing the term 'galácticos' (meaning superstars in Spanish) to symbolise their ambition to dominate their sport with the best players in the world. Yet, athletes can become problematic in terms of positioning because they increasingly come and go from teams, taking their reflected star power with them on their personal journeys. LeBron James, a modern branding phenomenon in his own right given his social media presence, is a champion basketballer in the NBA. Much in the way of Muhammad Ali, James is not averse to embracing the spotlight. 'King James,' as the player appears on social media,[14] has had successful playing stints at three NBA clubs, including twice at the Cleveland Cavaliers and also at the Miami Heat and Los Angeles Lakers. James' branding reached widespread recognition in 2010, when, as an unrestricted free agent, he participated in a nationally televised show, called 'The Decision,' to announce which club he would be moving to next.

For other teams, the athletes they choose can be much lower key, but still signal something critical about their positioning. One of the most famous examples is that of the Oakland Athletics Major League Baseball team of the early part of this century. They used advanced statistical analysis (a process later referred to as 'Moneyball' in a best-selling book[15] and Hollywood movie) to recruit undervalued players who combined to make the team highly successful for a relatively low wages bill. In that case, despite not winning the ultimate prize – the World Series – the Athletics managed to position themselves as shrewd operators who understood the complexities of the economics of sport better than other teams. The approach not only attracted fans and sponsors, eager to be cast in a similar light of 'outsmarting the opposition,' but players who also realised that the team had built a culture away from dominating individual personalities.

Sport brands can use positioning in numerous ways to further their branding ambition. Virtually anything can serve as a positioning platform if it can be leveraged with authenticity, if it can resonate with truth and value to a target audience, and if the attribute is meaningful in the context of rival brands. Nike, despite its global success and wide range of products, tries to remain at its heart a running shoe company, sponsoring events around its home state of Oregon in the United States. Adidas made its mark as a football boot company and leapt to fame through its association with the FIFA World Cup, a relationship it cherishes as symbolic of its history and authenticity. Formula One positions itself as the sport that leads technology and innovation; golf is portrayed as the sport for corporates and professionals; cycling is increasingly portraying itself as the sport of the people given its universal application to human movement in environmentally friendly ways; and boxing is fighting to re-establish its position as a pure form of sport competition given numerous concerns about the dangers it poses to participants and the appeal of a range of other combat sports.

Positioning operates as a function of exposure and experience. As consumers begin to associate attributes with brand elements – be they colours, names, or other forms of association – a form of learning through repetition occurs. For many consumers, the aforementioned Ferrari brand might resonate with strong emotions like power and exhilaration, even though most fans will never drive one of their cars at all, let alone at high speed. Such exposure and experience, even if devoid of actual use, inspires links with classical conditioning, which describes physiological responses to circumstances wherein a conditioned stimulus and an unconditioned stimulus become paired. Ferrari is constantly referred to as highly desirable, reinforcing its perception of the dream driving experience. Arguably the most famous example of conditioning is psychologist Pavlov's study where the presence of food (unconditioned stimulus) and the sound of a metronome (conditioned stimulus) were paired to produce salivation (a conditioned response) in dogs. The classical conditioning concept has been demonstrated to exist in the preferences of consumers too.[16]

Conditioning as a sport branding mechanism

To be successful, sport branding must render in consumers' minds meaningful links between the brand (and its products) and a suite of associations. How then are these associations established, reinforced, and maintained over time? As we alluded to earlier, the answer comes in the form of conditioning.

The simplest way of looking at conditioning is based on exposure.[17] Repeated exposure to the pairing of poignant words and pleasing imagery or sounds with a product or brand engenders an emotional response sufficient to condition liking and preference without awareness.[18] That means, consumers do not consciously notice that their perceptions about a brand are being shaped through these connective communications.

A more complicated theory gives greater credit to consumers who may be well aware of the constant brand messages they are exposed to.[19] Attitudes towards brands are filtered through existing beliefs. A more cognitive (thought) heavy view of conditioning like this depicts consumers as information processors who use what they already believe to interpret branding stimuli. Conversely, the incoming stimuli nudge existing beliefs too. A critical implication emerging from the reciprocal effect is that brand associations meld into memory, slowly becoming connected with former perceptions and influencing future ones. When conditioning works, it is due to a successful anchor between what a consumer already likes and the brand associations they confer upon its products.[20] Sport brands hook on to existing preferences and wiggle their way into deeper attitudes. Emotive branding stimuli can still play a role too, amplifying the effect mainly by massaging attention.

Conditioning through brand associations

Understanding the nature of conditioning has proven advantageous to branding for savvy sport marketers, particularly given the limited time that consumers spend making purchasing decisions in online and retail environments such as team merchandise websites and apparel stores. Accordingly, brand elements play a prominent role towards increasing the probability that sport consumers will (a) be aware of a sport brand, (b) consider that brand (assuming awareness), and (c) choose that brand (assuming awareness and consideration).

A central factor in conditioning – as consumers accumulate automatic cognitive responses to association cues presenting as brand elements – is the physical as well as the mental impact that comes with it. For example, humans have been shown to have physiological responses to some branding elements, including textures and shapes of packaging, smells, and colour. So-called cool colours (e.g., blue) and pastel shades have been shown to have calming effects, while warm colours (e.g., red) stimulate and arouse.[21] Elements conferring physiological effects infuse every part of the marketing delivery system from websites to retail outlets where experiences can be affected in subtle ways. For example, a dietary and nutritional supplements store might use a combination of white and metallic colours to signify a clinical, laboratory-like, contemporary or futuristic atmosphere. Apparel stores often use white and black to create an elegant and uncluttered shopping environment that does not compete with the bright, eye-catching merchandise. Of course, sporting teams and clubs tend to dress their websites, social media, club rooms, and merchandise outlets in their playing colours. Some teams are also anecdotally said to make the visitor changing rooms as unappealing as possible in an aesthetic sense, in the hope that the impact on mood might affect the playing performance of their opposition.

As we have explained, the whole point of conditioning – and for that matter branding in general – is for brand elements to become associated with a particular sporting enterprise and/or its products through exposure, repetition, and experience. An investment in conditioning constitutes an investment in brand value. Successfully associate a brand with the right words, designs, styles, or other brand elements – and consumers will come to the party.

Fifty years ago, Manchester United was not well known to most sport fans for any sustained periods of sporting success, having even been relegated to the second level of English football in 1974. Today, the club exemplifies the power of conditioning as a branding weapon. For Manchester United, some of their branding legacy must be attributed to a horrific aircraft accident that occurred in Munich in 1958, killing eight players and wounding several others who would never play again. That team, having been champions of England in both preceding years, was known as the 'Busby Babes,' named for their youthful exuberance and the manager Matt Busby, who himself was badly hurt in the accident. The accident garnered international attention, putting a club from the north of England on the map as the world shared in their grief.[22] United understandably wallowed in the years that followed, before winning the European Cup in 1968. From there, however, it would be another three decades before they returned to a European Cup Final, spending many of those years watching as arch-rival Liverpool went on its golden run of English titles, building its famous brand legacy.

Despite the relative lack of success by their ambitiously lofty standards, Manchester United remained synonymous with the attractive, attacking football of the 'Busby Babes' throughout the 1970s and 1980s. When championship success returned to the club in the 90s, its brand was renowned for resilience, style, and a narrative that provided a potent branding blend of redemption that captured the hearts and minds of followers all around the globe. With the birth of the English Premier League (EPL) in 1992, Manchester United went on to win 13 of the first 21 titles, a relentless rate of success that allowed them to firmly establish a global brand, adorned with superstars such as David Beckham, a worldwide array of sponsor brands wishing to bask in the reflected glory, and a manager in Sir Alex Ferguson who understood the power of the media and how it could be used to shape the image of his team. The sum of Manchester United's parts came to reflect success with unerring consistency, conditioning sport fans that the team represented the epitome of sport branding.

Manchester United was fortunate that its greatest period of success propelled an immense increase in the exposure of the team through the popular media just at the time when global communications through the Internet also took off. In turn, sport consumers the world over became unmistakably aware of the Manchester United juggernaut, a simple by-product of exposure frequency, combined with a suite of favourable associations, helpfully linking the red club to success both on and off the field. That is not to suggest that the club's brand development was simply good fortune or merely the consequence of a sustainable period of success. Getting a product to a position of strong brand awareness requires considerable promotion (and as a consequence, large budgets), and/or the strategic use of cues (such as a logo, slogan, character, colour, mnemonic device, etc.) that help maintain elevated levels of brand recognition. As long as brand elements remain uniquely linked to the brand, are well distributed and known, and create well-designed associations, the conditioning effects will prove favourable. In short, conditioning from a branding viewpoint demands long-term efforts to educate consumers about a connection between brand elements and the brand name. As we will explore in the following chapter on leveraging brands, effective conditioning builds a brand's capital in the form of brand value or equity that comes together with consistency and synergy.

A consistency amongst parts proves critical in marketing as consumers will be the first to notice anything that does not 'make sense.' Where inconsistencies appear, a consumer is likely to be left confused or with the need to create a decision-making shortcut to try and reach a satisfactory solution or explanation. For example, if a consumer were navigating through their favourite online sporting merchandise site and decided to buy an item, but the 'click to purchase' button was red instead of green, they might have good reason to pause. The colour green universally denotes 'proceed,' while red signals 'stop.' In recent years as Manchester United has failed to live up to its earlier successful exploits, fans around the world have looked for inconsistencies in its branding as an explanatory variable, including claims that the club has become too revenue-driven and purchased the wrong types of star players. Observers in this case have been noting incongruity between the brand of Manchester United as one of unerring and elite success, and performances in recent years where even making the top four in the EPL, and the resultant qualification for the lucrative Champion's League, has proven difficult.

The linkage and association recall process in putting together the pieces of a brand puzzle operate seamlessly when it makes intuitive sense to sport consumers. Thus, airlines generally identify their planes with a logo on the tailfin, car manufacturers place badge markings on the rear trunk and on or near the front grille of their vehicles, and sport shoe brands emblazon the sides of their shoes with distinct markings, such as adidas' three stripes or Nike's 'swoosh.' When something is out of place – at least in the minds of consumers – such as a shoe without a logo, a plane with an unadorned tailfin, or a brand like Manchester United not having a pool of successful superstars – something can feel amiss. For a consumer, brand disparity is unsettling, leading them to potentially look elsewhere to make sense of what is happening. This can chip away at the value of a brand. Although some sport teams like Manchester United enjoy enormous resilience to see them through tough times, it is not always the case with sporting brands, where fickle interests from sponsors, the media, and other stakeholders can prove unfavourable. One only has to look at the sporting market in the United States, where teams move from city to city regularly. Nothing can be taken for granted in sport, or branding. Both require disciplined patience and consistency for success.

Conclusion – elegant elements

In this section, we reinforced the importance of integrated marketing communications, consumer learning, and a brand's willingness to invest the time, resources, and energy in building associations with strong, unique, and favourable elements. A brand element comes to be linked with a sport brand in the minds of consumers if it establishes the patterns, contact points, and resonance that embed appropriate associations.

For busy sport consumers trying to make sense of product offerings amongst a proliferation of messages and competition, choices can quickly become too complex for comfort. In response, clever brands help to simplify their messages; products and associated advertising need to be striking, simple, and engaging. Typically, marketing communications and products will contain distinct brand elements to assist in this process.

The concept of associations requires an understanding of consumer behaviour, as for brands and brand elements to be associated with a product or sporting enterprise, the brand owner must recognise its consumer base (i.e., actual and potential purchasers or users of its product/s) as well as understand how consumers go about the buying process. As a result, brand custodians can develop appropriate, tailored marketing solutions suitable to condition consumers to be aware of, and recall their brand, with minimal prompting – an outcome achieved through repetitive exposure as well as through effective usage and communication of the brand and its elements.

In summary, brands and their brand elements help consumers in the buying decision process by removing some of the risk in decision-making. This is achieved through consumer learning. Consumers come to accept attributes, associations, and information through usage of a product and/ or integrated marketing communications. Learning can be intentional or unintentional because it occurs as a consequence of conditioning.

Notes

1 Maese, R. (2016). *The one tattoo that only we can get: Olympians put some skin in the Games*. Retrieved from https://www.washingtonpost.com/ sports/olympics/the-one-tattoo-that-only-we-can-get-olympians-put-some-skin-in-the-games/2016/08/04/983be0ea-5a41-11e6-9aee-80759 93d73a2_story.html?noredirect=on&utm_term=.b64dfa403f7c.
2 International Olympic Committee (2018). *Generation games: How the IOC is working to evolve the Olympic Games for the next generation of athletes and fans*. Retrieved from https://www.olympic.org/news/generation-games-how-the-ioc-is-working-to-evolve-the-olympic-games-for-the-next-generation-of-athletes-and-fans.
3 International Olympic Committee (2016). *IOC approves five new sports for Olympic Games Tokyo 2020*. Retrieved from https://www.olympic.org/ news/ioc-approves-five-new-sports-for-olympic-games-tokyo-2020.
4 Engel, J.F., Blackwell, R.D., & Kollat, D.T. (1978). *Consumer Behavior*. Hinsdale, IL: Dryden Press.
5 Pegoraro, A.L., Ayer, S.M., & O'Reilly, N.J. (2010). Consumer consumption and advertising through sport. *American Behavioural Scientist, 53*, 1454–1475.
6 Stavros, C., Meng, M., Westberg, K., & Farrelly F. (2014). Understanding fan motivation for interacting on social media. *Sport Management Review, 17*(4), 455–469.
7 Jones, I. (2000). A model of serious leisure identification: The case of football fandom. *Leisure Studies, 19*, 283–298; Wiley, C.G., Shaw, S., & Havitz, M. (2000). Men's and women's involvement in sports: An examination of the gendered aspects of leisure involvement. *Leisure Sciences, 22*(1), 19–31.

8 Cornwell, T.B., & Coote, L. (2005). Corporate sponsorship of a cause: The role of identification in purchase intent. *Journal of Business Research, 58*, 268–276.

9 Fink, J., Trail, G., & Anderson, D. (2002). An examination of team identification: Which motives are most salient to its existence? *International Sports Journal, 6*(2), 195–207.

10 Carlzon, J. (1987). *Moments of Truth*. Cambridge, MA: Ballinger.

11 Belch, G.E., & Belch, M.A. (1999). *Advertising and Promotion: An Integrated Marketing Communications Perspective*. Boston, MA: McGraw-Hill.

12 International Paralympic Committee (2017). *Brand book*. Retrieved from https://www.paralympic.org/sites/default/files/document/17080109581 7878_2017_07%2BIPC%2BBrand%2BBook.pdf.

13 McDonnell, J. (2019). AFL prepares to rebrand, begins work on new logo. Retrieved from http://www.adnews.com.au/news/afl-prepares-to-rebrand-begins-work-on-new-logo.

14 See https://www.instagram.com/kingjames/?hl=en and https://twitter.com/KingJames.

15 Lewis, M. (2004). *Moneyball: The Art of Winning an Unfair Game*. New York: Norton.

16 Bierley, C., McSweeney, F.K., & Vannieuwkerk, R. (1985). Classical conditioning of preferences for stimuli. *Journal of Consumer Research, 12* (Dec), 316–323; Gorn, G.J. (1982). The effects of music in advertising on choice behaviour: A classical conditioning approach. *Journal of Marketing, 46* (Winter), 94–101.

17 Zajonc, R.B. (1980). Feeling and thinking: Preferences need no inferences. *American Psychologist, 35*(2), 151–175.

18 Cornwell, T.B., Weeks, C.S., & Roy, D.P. (2005). Sponsorship-linked marketing: Opening the black box. *Journal of Advertising, 34*(2), 22–42.

19 Priluck, R., & Till, B.D. (2004). The role of contingency awareness, involvement and need for cognition in attitude formation. *Journal of the Academy of Marketing Science, 32*(3), 329–344.

20 Keller, K.L. (2003). Brand synthesis: The multidimensionality of brand knowledge. *Journal of Consumer Research, 29*, 596–600.

21 Grossman, R.P., & Wisenblit, J.Z. (1999). What we know about consumers' color choices. *Journal of Marketing Practice: Applied Marketing Science, 5*(3), 78–88.

22 Morrin, S.R. (2007). *The Munich Air Disaster*. Dublin: Gill & Macmillan.

4 Leveraging sport brands

Introduction – measuring the benefits

The association between strong brands and commercial success seems intuitive, but the relationship has also been demonstrated through objective studies.[1] For sport brand owners, the key lies with cultivating a suite of brand elements – or even just a single critical one – that gains an automatic and indefatigable niche in sport consumers' minds. A wide range of benefits have been associated with robust brand elements, including improved perceptions of product performance, greater consumer loyalty, less vulnerability to competitive marketing actions, less exposure to marketing crises, larger margins, more inelastic consumer response to price increases, more elastic consumer response to price decreases, greater trade cooperation and support, increased marketing communications effectiveness, possible licensing opportunities, and additional brand extension opportunities.[2] Strong brand elements demonstrably underpin successful brand outcomes in every area that can be measured.

Accordingly, the association of a sport brand, or its brand elements, with a sport enterprise can prove immensely valuable. If legally protected, brand owners can invest and develop their brand offerings and then reap the benefits of their assets. As a result, sport athletes (e.g., Serena Williams; Conor McGregor), businesses (e.g., Under Armour; Ferrari), events (e.g., Olympic Games; FIFA World Cup), and teams (e.g., FC Barcelona; Dallas Cowboys) have tremendous value tied up in what accountants describe as goodwill. Valuations of goodwill (as opposed to just tangible assets) accrue due to high levels of brand awareness and favourable brand attitudes. Combined, the two make sporting brands valuable because they simplify consumer decision-making; they provide fans with a sense of security that gives them the means to buy, trust, and use preferred brands with confidence,[3] and signal a certain level of quality, thereby encouraging those consumers who have bought a product and found it satisfactory, to repurchase.[4]

Building a strong sporting brand with high levels of consumer loyalty in the contemporary sporting market remains complicated and challenging. Consequently, strong sport brands represent tremendously valuable assets to sport enterprises that have been able to develop favourable, enduring, and unique associations between their brands and consumers over a period. As we introduced earlier, the brand value concept is typically referred to as 'brand equity,' but it all begins with brand awareness, which can be measured through brand recognition and brand recall, as we shall explain next.

Brand awareness

Consumer awareness is critical in all forms of marketing as without it no knowledge can form. You cannot know anything about something you are unaware of, let alone like it enough to buy. In the sporting context, a consumer must, of course, be able to identify a brand with some clarity in order to make a deliberate purchase or to form some type of valuable relationship. Clarity becomes decisive should the consumer choose to make a repeated purchase of the same brand. Brand managers seek to specify and measure the awareness that their products and brands command, and have devised the concept of brand recognition, and, even better, brand recall, to help measure consumers' propensity to make an initial identification and then associate it with explicit brand elements.

Everything starts with awareness. At this point, a brand can choose whether to aim for a foundational level of recognition – having their brand appropriately recognised when consumers come into contact with some part of it – or strive for recall, a much more difficult objective as it involves unaided recollection. One point to keep in mind is that brand awareness is causally linked to investment. The more money and effort infused into generating awareness, the greater the likelihood that awareness will eventuate from the exposure generated, and indeed multiply, as media sources and individuals pass on the message. Almost every person in the world, for example, knows who the president of the United States is given the enormous exposure that comes with this role. For many sporting brands, athletes, and events, the inherent global interest in their actors and actions can also elevate awareness rapidly – from the latest tennis Grand Slam champion to the team who upset the favourites in a major football match.

For many brands, sport has paved a pathway to rapid awareness, thanks to the exposure (and associated interest) it can generate. Nothing is a better exemplar of this than the annual Super Bowl in the United States, that pits the two leading teams in the NFL in the ultimate game to determine that season's champion team. The Super Bowl was first played in 1967, and grew rapidly to establish itself as a giant sporting brand in its own right. The Super Bowl's power as a brand comes from its gravitas symbolising the showdown of the best teams in the most popular sport in the USA, and is celebrated in a festive atmosphere, moving from city to city each season in a supreme display of corporate power.

The NFL, arguably the most successful sporting brand on the planet, treats the Super Bowl as its prized product by emphasising the status and cultural symbolism that elevates it to the most celebrated sporting day in the country's crowded entertainment calendar. The game draws attention from around 100 million viewers on television in the USA (and many more around the world) who not only follow the exploits of the players, but also the corporate brands that have paid breath-taking sums to punctuate the game with television commercials. These advertisements, of which there are around 90 for each game, consume one hour of broadcast time and come at the cost of around US$5 million for each 30-second spot.[5] The vast array of advertisers who choose to pay this sum, and the many millions more to create an ad suitable for use in each spot, understand the enormous awareness that such exposure can deliver.[6] One Super Bowl ad may be enough for a brand to leave an indelible mark on its target audience, as Apple did when they launched their Macintosh computer with the iconic and Orwellian '1984' campaign that aired in that year.

While it is likely that most sport aficionados will have heard of the Super Bowl, the annual game does not quite reach the status of two events that have come to define sport branding in our generation. These are, of course, the IOC's Olympic Games, which are held every two years through a rotation of summer and winter events, and the FIFA World Cup, the pinnacle quadrennial world football championship. Both the Olympic Games and the FIFA World Cup make fascinating studies in sport branding, given the global awareness they command is an astonishingly powerful mechanism for sponsoring brands to use for leverage. However, the branding success of these events has been no simple or inevitable path to glory. Both the IOC and FIFA worked relentlessly to rescue the brand value of their events over the years as crisis threatened to derail them. For the IOC, it was the summer games of Los Angeles in 1984 that first put the event on a commercially profitable path, while FIFA has battled hard for commercial credibility amid allegations of corruption among some of its officials and associates over recent years.[7] Both brands have now emerged supreme in power and awareness, with products that not only enjoy immense awareness, but are also commercial benchmarks in how branding and marketing operate. For many sport brands and associated stakeholders, however, the sheer magnitude of events like the Super Bowl, Olympics, and World Cup remains well beyond reach. How then can they hope to build brand awareness through recognition and recall, and what does each entail?

Brand recognition

If a consumer can accurately report that they are familiar with a brand when brand elements or the product itself is presented, then it may be said that brand awareness has been achieved. In essence, brand recognition means being able to establish what category a brand belongs to when presented with one or more of its brand elements (e.g., a brand name, logo, symbol, character, spokesperson, slogan, jingle, packaging, colour, or creative style). For example, a consumer might notice a narrow aluminium can emblazoned with a red-coloured logo comprising a stylised bull and horns, and immediately recognise the Red Bull brand and link this to the category of energy drink. Or, a consumer might observe Cristiano Ronaldo wearing a shirt with black and white stripes and immediately connect the superstar player to the Italian football team Juventus. When brand recognition has been achieved, a consumer will associate the positives of identifiable brand elements back to the brand, which will then link to the category. This is a common ambition for marketers because it allows them to build identifiable icons that can be more readily placed in the minds of consumers than just a brand name alone. For all brands, recognition represents a foundational aim. Without at least brand recognition, the brand journey terminates.

Brand recall

Brand recall refers to an aggregate proportion of consumers who recollect a brand unaided when prompted by the mention of a product category. Brand recall can be tested by stating a category and then noting which brands are mentioned or recalled and in what order this occurs. For example, if the category 'running shoe' is mentioned, a consumer might be able to name several brands that come to mind without being prompted, such as adidas, New Balance, and Asics. But when the category 'basketball shoe' is introduced, the same consumer might immediately name Nike.

Only a limited number of brands in a category can achieve brand recall. High levels of brand recall among consumers is obviously highly desirable for a brand owner as it evidences the kind of strong bond between category and brand that should lead to sales. Which brand is 'top of mind' – the brand first thought of when the category is highlighted – becomes especially relevant when considering brand recall. Achieving top-of-mind awareness can be a function of a large marketing budget that delivers access to prime communication platforms, often during major sporting events such as the Super Bowl, as well as the chance to repeat the message regularly, known in marketing terms as 'maximising frequency.'

The partner to frequency is known as 'reach,' which refers to the number of people exposed to a piece of marketing communication. Reach is valuable in marketing and branding as it helps measure whether sufficient numbers of people are exposed to a message. A trade-off between reach and frequency might be required, however, as the search for new people to expose a message to might come at the cost of the opportunity to repeat messages to those who have already heard it. You might wonder why a message should be repeated, but keep in mind that marketing is a competitive game and staying present in the mind of a consumer means repeating messages over and over, particularly when a brand has limited recognition or is trying to beat rivals and achieve a higher rate of recall. Brands in all categories must balance the tricky tension between reach and frequency, particularly because many sporting brands rely on partnerships with media organisations to facilitate their messaging requirements. Resolving the tension demands that sporting brands become creative in seeking maximum reach and the opportunity to amplify frequency.

A magnificent example of brand awareness in sport is that of Brazilian football icon Pelé, one of the most famous athletes of all time. At the 1970 FIFA World Cup Final, seconds before the start of the match, Pelé appeared to ask the referee to delay his opening whistle so he could adjust his boot laces. The resultant pause to tie his shoes was captured on close-up by a television camera, which beamed the Puma brand logo on the side of his shoe to hundreds of millions of fans across the globe as they eagerly waited for the match to commence. For Puma, the moment yielded reach of priceless value; at precisely the most opportune moment, Pele's action reminded the world of Puma's connection to one of the greatest players of all time.[8]

Brand personality

As part of the ambition to cultivate distinctive and differentiated products and services, sport marketers try to infuse their brands with human-like characteristics, in the process amplifying their emotional appeal and personal relatability. Just as with an individual's personality, brands might be said to possess personalities too. In fact, the concept of brand personality has imported numerous ideas from personality psychology theories in order to help express consumers' relationships with brands.[9] Here, the key assumption is that much can be learnt about a consumer's brand perceptions if the brand itself is treated like another person with a unique personality. A suite of brand personality assessment tools has emerged. Most treat brand personality much like individual personality, using derivatives of the familiar openness, conscientiousness, extraversion, agreeableness, and neuroticism scales. For example, the most influential version begins with five components: sincerity (down-to-earth, honest, wholesome, cheerful); excitement (daring, spirited, imaginative, up-to-date); competence (reliable, intelligent, successful); sophistication (upper class, charming); and ruggedness (outdoorsy, tough).[10] By employing scales with this much detail, consumer impressions can be mapped, interpreted, and tracked by vigilant brand managers.

It is possible, even likely, that brand personality might be confused with classical dimensions of product performance. For example, a yoga apparel product might be viewed as 'sensuous,' or a sport's drink 'energetic.' The degree to which these associations are misleading is unclear. Sport provides a further example in that, unlike more mundane products such as dishwashing liquid or salt, sport is inherently exciting, unpredictable, and built around a desirable contest. It is precisely this kind of imagery that attracts corporate brands to sponsorship arrangements in the hope that some of it might rub off. The inherent properties of a product, whether sport or salt, are likely to influence a consumer's view of the brand. From a practical viewpoint, it does not matter whether a consumer is influenced by the functionality of the product itself. What matters are the personality traits that they employ to describe the brand, irrespective of their catalyst.

Attempts to attribute human characteristics to inanimate entities like brands have proven sufficiently advantageous to warrant continued use, with a couple of cautions. To begin with, the cultural specificity of certain aspects of personality need to be considered. These would mainly involve the effect of value and social judgements. For example, geographical, ethnic, religious, and sporting cultures all play a role in influencing brand personality assessments; what is compelling in one locale may be repellent in another. However, it might be argued that the culture in which a sport brand has become embedded is relative anyway, and its reflection in brand personality outcomes is simply a contextual reference. The precise impact of cultural context on brand personality is obviously more important for sport brands operating in the global market. It should also be remembered that the whole concept of brand personality – like most branding ideas – emerged based on the experiences of brands operating in Western, developed regions, especially the USA.

Descriptors of human personality often convey different meanings when applied to different sport brands; a reflection of the inherent complications in artificially layering human characteristics over inanimate brands. Also, the degree of social identification between the consumer and product / brand is influential in the construction of brand personality and the subsequent meaning attached to a sport brand. Thus, the interaction between a sport brand and its consumers is a dynamic process mired in personal identity and social meaning. As a result, sport brands are potentially even more rigidly fixed to their personalities than other brands.

It is important to remain aware of the symbolic nature of brands and the implications of attributing human-like characteristics to them. For example, what if the sport brand possesses a characteristic that is not well described by a human feature, or if the feature in a human would be considered negative but is advantageous in sport (e.g., ruthless, aggressive, domineering)? Thus, it is important to consider the characteristics displayed within the context of the sport brand itself. Nevertheless, sporting brands often look to capitalise on strong characteristics in order to provide a marketing platform for their products. The Hawthorn Football Club in the Australian Football League proudly proclaims itself to be the 'Family Club,' while teams in the English Premier League, such as Manchester United, have, in recent years, been accused of being too corporate and soulless for a team that sprang from the roots of a working-class city in England's north. A decade ago, when the commercialisation of Manchester United meant a heavily indebted balance sheet, many fans attended home games sporting scarves in the green and gold colours of Newton Heath, the long defunct team from the Carriage and Wagon department of the Lancashire and Yorkshire Railways from which Manchester United was founded. The message to United's American owners was simple. The fans felt the brand belonged to them, not to the stock market or a corporate entity.

Brand attitude

Brand attitude, as we have briefly discussed, summarises a consumer's thoughts and feelings concerning their overall evaluation of a brand in relation to its ability to meet the motivations that stimulated the purchase in the first place. Attitude (which is sometimes referred to as brand image) can be measured in relation to competitors and usually has both cognitive (thinking) and affective (feeling) components. Cognitive aspects of attitude are those relating to knowledge, beliefs, and reason, while affective elements of attitude refer to emotions and feelings.[11]

A consumer's attitude to a brand can vary over time, influenced by a range of factors including previous experiences, word-of-mouth, advertising, point-of-sale promotional material, and social media influencers. Some factors may be outside the control of a marketer, such as country-of-origin effects (e.g., the perception that German sports cars are well built) or the marketing activities of competitors in the category (e.g., price setting in a highly competitive industry such as sports supplements).

Brand equity and value

As marketing and branding have become more sophisticated, brand owners have sought more nuanced ways of measuring the value that their brands have accrued. As a result, brand equity, as we explained in Chapter 2, has become a popular concept to define a brand's inherent value. We return to the brand equity concept here because it helps to unlock the leveraging impact that a sport brand can wield, giving it the power to not only perform but also to attract an array of other brands that might wish to be associated with it. Take, for example, the Super Bowl. Its equity is immense, having been infused with meaning far more valuable than a mere football game.

Part of brand equity's appeal as a measure is that it can provide a useful depiction of a brand's full value including the return on investment that accompanies consumers' psychological commitments, as well as a predictive insight into a brand's future earning capacity. Thus, brand equity holds importance not only for financial reasons (i.e., the value accrued to a strong brand) but also for psychological reasons (i.e., the value that is inherently intangible and exists in the minds of various stakeholders).

Brand equity can be a bit tricky to capture, considering it aims to embrace the entire psychological disposition of a brand's potentially fickle consumers. In principle, the measure derives from the extent to which consumers know a brand, and subsequently what they feel about it as a result. For instance, positive brand equity will be demonstrated by consumers' familiarity with a brand as well as the favourable, strong, and unique associations that go with it, packed deeply in the mind and automatically retrieved on cue as necessary. As we have noted, associations drive perceptions, feelings, and preferences in ways that determine what value a brand accumulates for its owner.

Because of their ability to influence consumer purchasing behaviour, brand associations are valuable to companies seeking to forge a link between their products and certain characteristics. For example, when faced with the choice of tennis racquet from a leading brand such as Wilson, and with a brand from an unknown manufacturer, a consumer who chooses the former is expressing positive understanding and appreciation of the chosen brand, even if the products are functionally similar. Preferences can stem from experience, advertising messages, or symbolic associations with the brand elements, in this case from such influences as athlete endorsements, colour, styling, logo, or perceived value. As a general principle, the difference consumers are willing to pay between the known brand and the unknown brand reflects the known brand's positive equity, and thus becomes measurable.

As we have noted, it is also possible to take brand equity and its components further by distinguishing between corporate brand equity and individual brand equity. For example, the United Arab Emirates- and Chinese-owned City Football Group, possesses negligible brand equity in the sense of consumer psychological commitment. In fact, few football fans would recognise the name City Football Group. However, most football fans would be well aware of the football brands the company owns, like Manchester City Football Club. Even when corporate and individual brands are well known and paired together, they can take on a different meaning. Consider the aforementioned FIFA World Cup. For many brands (and consumers), the value in the FIFA brand is somewhat limited given its connection to the governing body, which has faced a well-publicised period of intense scrutiny in the past decade. The World Cup itself though is resplendent in appeal and glory, providing FIFA with an almost impenetrable brand shield that generates not only enormous amounts of cash, but also remarkable passion.

The same principle applies for sporting-related goods. Some are owned by little known holding companies or corporate conglomerations that focus on the equity of their product line brands. For example, chances are that many outdoor recreation enthusiasts have familiarity with outdoors brands such as The North Face, SmartWool, and Eagle Creek. But few would have heard of their parent company, the VF Corp, which also owns more than ten other well-known brands competing in the outdoor market. Others like sports broadcasting network ESPN offer a proliferation of products all under a single umbrella brand, even if their specific products also carry some name recognition like SportsCenter or Monday Night Football.

Ambush branding

Brand elements associated with a sporting brand are, as we have outlined, best built through integrated marketing communications, which usually necessitate high levels of expenditure to ensure that messages not only reach audiences, but are also repeated often enough to be recalled and/or recognised as being associated with a brand. At times, a sport enterprise might attempt to use an element or elements of a brand legitimately associated with a competitor, effectively misappropriating their associations in order to secure additional awareness, positive image reinforcement, or subsequent sales. In such instances, consumers mistakenly identify a brand or assume that there exists a commercial association between competing brands, when one did not exist, based upon the appearance of a common brand element or elements. The attempt might be described as ambush branding – appropriating a free ride by disingenuously signalling an association with another brand's already well-established brand elements.

In using the term 'free ride,' we mean that the ambushing competitor can obtain additional sales from consumer error and springboard off the positive associations attached to the established brand elements. In consequence, the free ride boosts consumers' perceptions of the imitator, allowing them to share in the positive associations that may exist with a brand element, without having to incur the expense (both in terms of time and money) connected with establishing positive associations to their own brand elements.

Not only can ambush branding assure the success of the competitive product, it also means that the attendant cost savings can be used to undercut the originator. Moreover, ambush branding diminishes the uniqueness of a brand element for the competitor that established the successful elements in the first place, thereby reducing the brand equity of the original brand.

Ambush branding can occur through mistakes in identification in the marketplace amongst consumers, or by simply depriving the initiating brand of a previously exclusive element that was fundamental to their product perception or integrated marketing communications strategy. Plentiful examples can be found in the sports and energy drink marketplace where many newer products have duplicated the first moving brand's drink container shape and styling, without actually coming close enough to infringe legal entitlements.

Legal distinctions are a critical consideration as the sport of branding and ambushing unfolds. Many people mistakenly think that ambushing is always illegal. However, the difference between what is acceptable and what is not is shrouded in grey area and copious amounts of interpretation. Most countries will not allow brands to engage in misleading or deceptive practices, and the appropriation of brand elements can fall under this legal umbrella. A sporting body anywhere in the world would be unlikely to call their final game of the season the 'Super Bowl,' for example, without expecting the legal wrath of the NFL. Similarly, the Los Angeles Lakers may not appreciate the use of their famous nickname by other teams, whether they are in basketball or not, as we have seen with the South Melbourne soccer team.

Other efforts might exhibit more subtlety and include just one similarity to a competitor's brand element. An event that uses the five Olympic rings, made famous by the Olympic Games logo and flag, would certainly not succeed. But what if they replaced the rings with squares, or reduced the number of rings to three, or increased them to six? Adidas, in the sports footwear category, which we discuss in more detail shortly, has faced challenges around the world as other shoe manufactures have used 'parallel stripes' on their shoes, leading courtroom judges to make decisions as to whether four stripes or two stripes, or even the distance between the stripes, have constituted breaches of trademark. Legal battles can often be long and full of nuanced complexity relating to local laws, customs, and practices.[12]

While brands can typically see the value in leveraging established branding concepts to maximise their impact, there is no simple solution in most cases, nor a simple set of guidelines that can be followed. For example, a brand designed in Switzerland might play upon perceptions of Swiss quality and expertise, benefiting from country-of-origin effects. The same brand could not use a Swiss star like Roger Federer in their promotion, however, unless they had explicit permission to do so. Using an image of Federer in an ad because he is Swiss is not acceptable either, as Federer has extensive image rights across the world, and any perception of his endorsement would require a legal contract.

While brands owners sensibly shy away from the risk of costly litigation, they nevertheless tend to feel a moral duty to defend their brands and seek to maximise opportunity when it exists. If a brand was to allow its main competitor free access to exploit a sporting event or association, stakeholders may construe this as a poor defensive marketing. In effect, by not seeking to disrupt the actions of a competitor, a brand might be allowing a rival to exercise its leverage with success. The challenge thus becomes one of knowing where to draw the line – maximising value for a brand without breaking the law. In a global world with local laws, dealing with ownership issues – especially of intangible ideas and brand personality traits – will only get more complex and difficult. No matter how experienced, brand managers are advised to seek specialist legal opinions before proceeding anywhere near what may be seen as ambush branding.

For sport brands, traversing the ambush and ownership tension can be defining since the power of a brand can be crushed if the elements that have been built up become freely useable by any competing organisation. Why pay to be a sponsor when being an ambusher is not only cheaper but also more flexible? Not surprisingly, sport brand elements have become some of the most protectable and stringently enforced in the world as brand owners seek to protect their investments. As we will explore in the following chapter, however, sometimes tightly controlling these brand elements can be counterproductive. In the world of the 'postmobile' consumer – who takes great care in curating their own brand experiences – sometimes giving up control and letting consumers build the brand experience is the wiser long-term strategy.

The case of sporting footwear

In order to integrate some of the critical concepts outlined so far, it is instructional to see how they embed within a special case and context. To that end, in the remainder of this chapter, we will use the case of sporting footwear brands as a way to explain how some key branding concepts translate into practice.

Let us begin with brand elements. After all, without brand elements such as logos and symbols, there can be no brand and thus no brand equity. Earlier, we outlined a lengthy list of brand benefits. All of these can readily accrue to companies owning brands in the sports footwear market through the development of suitable brand elements that obtain strong, unique, and favourable associations through sustained marketing efforts.

With the risk of understatement, the global sports footwear market can be described as highly competitive, with many large multinational brands competing on the basis of both function and fashion.

In competitive markets like the one containing the 'sneaker wars,'[13] branding and the role it plays becomes amplified as consumers must make choices from a wide variety of similar brands. Equally, the brand owners must work hard to establish their brands and communicate them successfully to the marketplace by somehow cutting through the immense clutter and advertising noise.

With specific regard to sports footwear, brand owners rely on successfully instilling their own unique brand elements into the consumer psyche. When it works, the benefits can include: ease of identification of their product by consumers; positive associations that are ascribed to brand elements by consumers such as authority, status, quality, trust, and reliability; transferability of the elements into new product types that would then give those new product types greater chance of success; and, a resultant enhancement of brand equity.

Sports footwear can prove difficult to classify as the products can serve both a functional and form requirement in consumers. They may be sought out for use by consumers who are motivated by the need for a practical solution, such as shoes used for playing sport. At the same time, sporting footwear can provide for a fashion need where consumers buy them to match casual outfits or to follow a particular style. Indeed, some consumers can be motivated by both function and form, and thus require a product that provides a sport-related function and looks good too. Leading brands in the sports footwear industry, such as Nike and adidas, seek to serve both requirements, either individually or simultaneously. Footwear giant adidas offers the case in point through an extensive footwear catalogue that includes highly specialist shoes designed principally for technical performance in a range of sports, in addition to carefully styled cross trainers intended for multipurpose casual use.

Understanding the consumers

A mixture of different, sometimes competing, consumer motivations can present a dilemma as brand managers tend towards one of two distinct approaches. The first deals with motivations from an 'informational' perspective, while the second takes a 'transformational' viewpoint.

An informational motivation infers that consumers enter the sports footwear category to mitigate a perceived problem (actual or potential) of some type, including dissatisfaction or cognitive conflict. For example, it might involve seeking out football boots to wear in a match, which will provide the requisite comfort, support, and protection, but not exceed a certain cost. A transformational motivation infers a more positive orientation towards a sense of pleasure or reward, such as social approval, sensual gratification, or intellectual stimulation.[14] Thus, a consumer might seek out a pair of shoes to match a certain fashion appearance that provides a sense of belonging within a social group or a sense of self-image or confidence.

Both motivations offer valid approaches for the sports footwear industry. Which one works best is largely dictated by the audience being targeted. Although brand managers would normally focus on one primary motivation in any given form of communication, an entire campaign will likely focus on both types of motivations in order to secure the advantages that go with each. For example, informational-motivated products (and branding) take a direct, or rational, style. The attributes, or problem-reducing elements, are presented simply, often in exaggerated form, to gain the attention and knowledge of the target audience with relative ease. In contrast, transformational-motivated products (and branding) take a more indirect, or emotional, style. The reward, or socially desirable elements of such a product, must be inferred by consumers who see the brand as something they would like to identify with on a personal level. Transformational communications tend to be more complex given their indirect nature and might require refinement to ensure that appropriate positive brand attributes are being accurately absorbed by the audience.

In the instance of sports footwear, regardless of whether an informational or transformational motivation exists, the presence of strong, recognisable brand elements such as logos and symbols allows the products to be more easily identified by consumers. Furthermore, the extended use of brand elements such as logos and symbols over a sustained period can lead to more than just ease of identification. It can instil positive associations with consumers who are prompted by the brand elements; the brand elements offer a 'short cut' to the positive feelings arising from consumers' repeated exposure to, and experience of, the product.

Brand transfer

Another branding benefit reaped by successful sports footwear companies arrives through what marketers call transferability. Strong brand elements, particularly those visually represented on the products like logos and symbols, seamlessly introduce consumers to new styles, ranges, and product types. As product design and innovation have become significant factors in marketing, the ability to readily transfer brand elements and values across new products has also emerged as a critical factor in brand longevity. Brand elements provide the springboard for transferability.

Logos and symbols take on an even greater importance in the sports footwear market because they constitute the elements most commonly considered part of a brand. They are closely linked to sports footwear in a physical and visual sense. All the other elements such as brand names and URLs, characters and spokespeople, slogans and jingles, packaging (including colour) and creative style are (with the exception of the brand name, which in itself can be a form of logo) typically more detached physically and visually from the product itself. While some footwear will also feature the brand name on the product, the logo or symbol declares the more common representation, which by its very placement and design is often more readily recognisable, particularly from distance.

In the sports footwear category, logos and symbols conventionally appear on the sides of shoes, between the sole and laces, given the need for visibility from numerous angles. For example, Nike's 'swoosh' logo, Asics' criss-cross pattern of stripes, New Balance's stylised 'N' design, and Puma's single, curved stripe all appear on the sides. Logos and symbols on sports footwear are carefully designed to be easily visible so as to stand out to consumers, who may be watching a sporting event, or who just notice them on other user's casual wear. Visibility comes through the use of distinct colours, styles, and designs that aim to attract attention and stick in the memory for later recognition.

Logos and symbols can also portray a decorative, fashion-orientated function given the prominence of their markings. A decorative function does not detract from the marketing functions of logos and symbols. In fact, it works hand-in-hand to ensure that what would otherwise be a plain and relatively standardised piece of footwear becomes something more important and distinct, whilst maintaining the brand equity that has been developed by a company.

Leveraging sport brands with sponsorship

To add another layer of complexity to the branding equation, a brand's role (and thus its associated brand elements) can be significantly enhanced through appropriate sponsorships. Sponsorship arrangements are essentially co-branding alliances, where the brand of a sponsor becomes integrated with that of the sponsored entity to produce marketing communication outcomes not easily obtained in other ways.

Many sporting goods manufacturers – and especially sports footwear companies – deploy an extensive range of sponsorships, including with individuals, teams, and events. These strategic alliances serve a broad range of marketing objectives, but always seek to enhance sponsor credibility and their product's performance. Further to these basic goals, if undertaken on an intensive global scale well-integrated into marketing communication efforts, sponsorship can embed a brand (and thus its associated elements) into popular culture. The process is amplified when the brand and its elements can be readily made visible to consumers, such as the application of logos to clothing, related apparel, and jewellery. It is, for example, a common occurrence to see people wearing clothing and related apparel from leading sportswear brands such as adidas and Nike that is clearly identified with key brand elements, such as the three-stripe mark in the case of adidas and the 'swoosh' logo in the case of Nike. Consumers come to expect that the unique branding marks will appear, not just as a form of identification, but as an integral part of the product itself. When it gets to this point, a brand has transcended traditional product–consumer relationships to reflect self-image and identity.

One example where adidas achieved some notable crossover of its footwear into pop culture occurred when renowned hip-hop musicians Run-D.M.C. released a song in 1986 entitled 'My Adidas' that included adidas shoes worn without laces.[15] Popular associations such as this one help brands like adidas escalate their status from consumer products to cultural icons. They also provide a powerful branding springboard to sell athletic clothing as fashionable garments.

A substantive sport sponsor, adidas' is one of just a handful of partners currently associated with FIFA, the world governing body of football and their quadrennial World Cup.[16] The tournament, as we have discussed, is perhaps the most significant event in the world for a sponsor to be aligned to given its global impact, cultural status, and commercial reach.[17]

Finally, we note that distinct branding marks, such as the adidas stripes, are not always immediately or automatically linked to positive attributes. Desirable associations must be created through a concerted investment and an understanding of markets and audiences. Again, as we have noted, branding does not happen by accident. Integrated branding works by arranging the pieces so that consumers can collect them in their minds and align them with their identities.

Conclusion – making a mark

Brand owners stand to gain considerable benefit when they successfully create associations between particular brand elements and their products. Brand elements represent the image and associated quality of the brand to customers, decorate the product to make it visually appealing, provide a launching pad for future endeavours, and, most importantly, enhance brand equity.

Strong sport brands yield benefits that can escalate exponentially over the length of their existence. As lower costs and higher returns accrue to strong brands, so too does brand value. This is because the longer customers remain brand loyal, the more profitable they become as a result of increased purchases, reduced operating costs, price premiums, and helpful referrals. In the next chapter, we take the branding process to a final stage in order to explain how all the various components of the process fit together to yield entities that can be bigger than the sum of their parts.

Notes

1 Kay, M.J. (2006). Strong brands and corporate brands. *European Journal of Marketing, 40*(7/8), 742–760.
2 Kotler, P., & Keller, K.L. (2006). *Marketing Management*. Upper Saddle River, NJ: Pearson.
3 Jacoby, J., Olson, J., & Haddock, R. (1971). Price, brand name, and product composition characteristics as determinants of perceived quality. *Journal of Applied Psychology, 55*(6), 570–579; Jacoby, J., Syzbillo, G., & Busato-Schach, J. (1977). Information acquisition behaviour in brand-choice situations. *Journal of Consumer Research, 3*(4), 209–216.
4 Erdem, T., & Swait J. (1998). Brand equity as a signaling phenomenon. *Journal of Consumer Psychology, 7*(2), 131–157.
5 Statista (2019). *Number and length of network TV commercials in the Super Bowl from 2003 to 2018*. Retrieved from https://www.statista.com/statistics/251588/number-and-length-of-network-tv-commercials-in-the-super-bowl/
6 Kim, K., & Cheong, Y. (2011). Creative strategies of Super Bowl commercials 2001–2009: An analysis of message strategies. *International Journal of Sports Marketing and Sponsorship, 13*(1), 2–17.
7 The United States Department of Justice (2015). *Nine FIFA Officials and Five Corporate Executives Indicted for Racketeering Conspiracy and Corruption*. Retrieved from https://www.justice.gov/opa/pr/nine-fifa-officials-and-five-corporate-executives-indicted-racketeering-conspiracy-and
8 Cronin, B. (2012). *Was Pele paid to tie his shoes during the 1970 World Cup final?* Retrieved from https://www.latimes.com/sports/la-xpm-2012-oct-15-la-sp-sn-pele-shoes-world-cup-20121015-story.html.
9 Seminal works include: Goldberg, L. (1990). An alternative description of personality: The big five factor structure. *Journal of Personality and Social Psychology, 59*(6), 1216–1229; Kassarjian, H. (1971). Personality and consumer behaviour: A review. *Journal of Marketing Research, 8*(1), 409–418; Norman, W. (1963). Toward an adequate taxonomy of personality attributes: Replicated factor structure in peer nomination personality ratings. *Journal of Abnormal and Social Psychology, 66*, 574–583; Oliver, J. (1990). The big five factor taxonomy: Dimensions of personality in the natural language and in questionnaires. In L.A. Pervn (Ed.), *Handbook of Personality: Theory and Research* (pp. 66–100). San Francisco, CA: Harper.

10 Aaker, J. (1997). Dimensions of brand personality. *Journal of Marketing Research, 34*(3), 347–356.

11 Schiffman, L., O'Cass, A., Paladino, A., & Carlson, J. (2013). *Consumer Behaviour*. Frenchs Forest, NSW: Pearson.

12 Jolly, J. (2019). *Adidas loses three-stripe trademark battle in European court*. Retrieved from https://www.theguardian.com/law/2019/jun/19/ adidas-loses-three-stripe-trademark-battle-in-european-court.

13 Smit, B. (2009). *Sneaker Wars*. New York: HarperCollins.

14 Rossiter, J.R., & Bellman, S. (2005). *Marketing Communications: Theory and Applications*. Frenchs Forest, NSW: Pearson.

15 Run-D.M.C. is widely acknowledged as one of the leading exponents of their musical style and has received numerous accolades and awards to support their status within this community.

16 See http://www.fifa.com/worldcup/organisation/partners/index.html for the list of partners and other commercial sponsors.

17 Flexibility refers to opportunities to expose or leverage the sponsorship association. As a comparison, the Olympic Games generally have more partners than the FIFA World Cup, but do not allow commercial signage in stadiums, thus limiting their value in comparison the FIFA World Cup.

5 Reinventing sport brands

Introduction – augmenting sport branding

Marketing plays an increasingly important part in sport business success, ensuring that the wants and needs of consumers (be they businesses or individuals) are identified and matched appropriately to the offerings provided in a marketplace. However, the world of branding is rapidly evolving, having stimulated a shift in the way some branding relationships have emerged, and consequently how value is perceived and measured. As a result, the notion of co-creating value has gained traction. It refers to a shared endeavour where consumers and producers interact synergistically with the aim of developing superior products that perfectly match the requirements of users. Working directly with consumers comes naturally to many sport brands. In this section, we explore co-creation in sport branding, and also briefly touch on the new type of consumer who has become the new normal, being both digitally literate and proactively engaged.

To cope with these changes and with an increasingly sophisticated and competitive business environment, we have witnessed the arrival and realignment of marketing support services designed to assist brands to better utilise available tools, and to provide strategic insights to assist with the planning, execution, and evaluation of marketing. Various forms of marketing services provide a valuable lever for sport branding, leading to improved opportunities for 'reinventing' sport brands and allowing them to flex in the turbulence of a cluttered and chaotic marketplace.

In this section, we also highlight how some support service options, channels, and media forms can affect the character of sport branding. Rather than create an inventory of the ever-swelling digital and social media channels that have become essential to deploying sport branding, we focus on the endgame; that is, what sport consumers are presented that represent a sporting brand. From there, we work backwards to reveal how all the elements, tools, and channels of sport branding meld to fashion a seamless and integrated outcome.

Co-creating sport branding

One of the fundamental changes to occur in branding in recent years has entailed a shift away from what a brand does with a consumer, towards what a consumer does with a brand in order to infer and drive value from the experience. This 'service-dominant logic'[1] focuses on creating brand experiences. Indeed, sport brands tend to be well placed to take advantage of the paradigm shift given that they inherently facilitate shared experiences with their customers as a fundamental part of their value proposition. In terms of co-branding (and perhaps part by accident and part by design), sport brands have become world leaders in cutting-edge branding approaches. Successful sport brands readily understand the new principle that great branding comes from ceding control to customers and allowing them to build and ascribe extra value through the experiences they participate in building.[2]

At its foundation, co-creation builds on the concept of engagement, asking the consumer to not just be a beneficiary of the product that they have purchased, but to actively contribute to the experience. The result discards traditional boundaries of producer and consumer – hence, the term 'prosumer,' which is sometimes used to identify the active role that customers can assume.[3] At a rudimentary level, any visitor to a high-level sporting event can quickly grasp the importance of co-creation. Fan engagement and enthusiasm feature central in the experience, from the most passionate of partisan fan right through to the casual 'theatregoer' who enjoys the atmosphere as much as the contest.

Leading sport brands have become somewhat enamoured with the concept of co-creation. They provide their fans not only with the permission to build the experience, but in many cases, the tools to do so as well. Consider Wilson, a sporting goods manufacturer from the USA that enjoys a long history of making high-quality equipment in a range of sports including tennis, baseball, basketball, and American football. Wilson is also well regarded for its golf equipment. In an effort to stimulate greater brand awareness of their golfing range, Wilson started a 'Driver versus Driver' reality show in 2016 that featured on the widely available and popular Golf Channel.[4] The series allowed consumers to design and build their own innovative golf drivers, with the winner's design converted into a marketable product to be sold by Wilson. The event was such a success that Wilson ran a second, even more popular series in 2018, which culminated in the winning 'Cortex' driver going on sale worldwide to considerable acclaim.

As the Wilson case exemplifies, co-creation leads to an elevation in brand equity that is effectively crowdsourced. Whatever economic, social, and symbolic values that are infused through intense shared partnerships with consumers go well beyond what brands have traditionally established with one-way approaches. Three intertwined themes emerge that all brands can use as a framework to traverse the co-creation journey. First, incessantly co-creating value with consumers; second, offering brands as 'clubs' of exclusive belonging; and third, harvesting emerging channels through which connection and identification can be both materialised and solidified.

One of the helpful developments for all brands in co-creation (but, in particular, sport brands given the fandom they tend to generate) is the newly arrived pre-eminence of a multitude of digital and mobile platforms through which consumers can engage. Where once traditional media required a one-way communication process, modern asynchronous channels across a variety of social media allow brands to listen in to their consumers and engage them in the brand building process on a continuous basis. Leading sport brands are zealous in tracking fan commentary, often allowing fans to take ownership of platforms. Perhaps no brand goes further than the NBA, which embraces social media as a complex system of platforms that allow fans to live the experience of the sport.[5] The NBA is similarly generous in giving fans access to tools in order to create highlights, engage with fellow fans, and reach out to star players. Leading sport brands have made consumers part of the brand through co-created experiences, delivering branding that remains relevant and meaningful to the people who matter most. Yet, at the same time, sport consumers have become increasingly demanding, aware that numerous entertainment experiences and options surround them, and that lifelong brand loyalty cannot be taken for granted no matter how much co-creation occurs.

The postmobile consumer and brand

While most sport brands occupy an advantageous branding position given their co-creation affinities and naturally loyal consumers, nothing can be taken for granted given the emergence of what has been labelled the 'postmobile' consumer,[6] who lives in a world where every device is connected to the cloud and every action is captured and analysed. In such a situation, the brand is aware of every movement a consumer makes, but the consumer too is aware of every branding action, giving themselves access to a ready supply of entertainment options competing relentlessly for their discretionary spending.[7] In consequence, sport brands will no longer be able to interrupt consumers with 'in-your-face' messaging. Consumers increasingly wield all the power, and therefore choose the level of interaction and individualisation that suits them. Powerful consumers mean that they will be highly selective about which brands they engage with and when. At the same time, consumers will easily be able to distinguish the brand offerings from competitors while enjoying seamless access to an array of new experiences. Why limit yourself to a small number of brands when you know exactly what is on offer from around the world? Postmobile consumers feel empowered to shape their experiences in a world where information is not just at their fingertips, but readily actionable into consumption decisions.

Who owns the brand of the future?

Early on in this book we commented that companies do not really own brands. Rather, it is consumers, through the summation of their feelings and experiences, who truly wield the power. While legally a brand can be protected, its worth (a term we have explained as equity) is wholly reliant on consumer action, making the consumer the real source of power. Although this axiom has always existed in marketing, it has become even more firmly entrenched with the rise of co-creation and postmobility. Another piece of the puzzle is the dazzling area of communication options that exist, ensuring that the modern brand is an entirely unique media experience. No longer are there simple channels to a target audience. Synergy and integration are critical, driving brand managers to seek multiple methods to reinforce their positioning and the ways experiences can be activated.

Reinventing sport brands through marketing services

Many sport enterprises employ outside marketing services to assist in the achievement of their marketing goals, and, as a result, they play a critical role in the 'reinvention' of sport brands. There is no requirement, legally or ethically, to use external marketing services, so the decision for brands is clearly one related to a perception that their own skills in one or more areas must be lacking or requiring some form of enhancement. Some sport enterprises want one-off assistance with a singular branding campaign, while others systematically work with marketing service providers to further their planning and execution activities.

The specific marketing services sought will vary greatly in terms of what a sport brand hopes to achieve. Marketing services can be necessary across a range of areas, often involving similar skills for different needs or junctures. For example, to pick 'design' as a service: in-store signage may require a designer; advice on packaging may require a designer; a website may require a designer; a piece of marketing collateral to hand to customers on the street may require a designer; a business card might require a designer; and so forth.

Providers of marketing services range significantly in size and style from individuals who can offer marketing services (and indeed it is a profession that typically requires no official accreditation or licensing system to do so), right through to multinational brands that have often developed their own systems and processes for providing guidance and assistance to clients. However, due to the fragmentation, specialisation, and dynamic nature of the sport market, online support to help deal with new forms of social media and digital technologies has become a standard practice.

Marketing services typically span three categories, although there is often considerable overlap and wide fragmentation within the categories themselves, as these services can occur across the spectrum of the marketing planning process: (1) research services – aimed at generating useful information, either from primary or secondary sources, that can help illuminate marketing options and desirable pathways; (2) communication services – aimed at fostering the connection and development of shared meaning between a brand and its target audience(s); and (3) planning and strategy services – aimed at providing branding guidance that is both sustainable and competitive.

Advertising services for sport branding

As advertising is clearly an important component of marketing in general and branding in particular, it stands to reason that while marketing services need not be advertising services, any advertising services will be (more broadly speaking) marketing services. Advertising services can be employed to help marketers navigate the complex pathways between brands and their consumers, ensuring that not only are suitable messages created and delivered, but that they also resonate with the larger branding picture that a sport enterprise is striving towards.

Advertising services are mainly sourced from 'agencies,' which also offer a wide array of inputs including strategy formulation, marketing research, media planning, design, evaluation, and messaging. Some agencies work from concept (working with the client on branding objectives) through to completion (the advertising appearing and being evaluated), while others may only deliver specific items (such as idea generation). However, not all advertising services providers are agencies. Any firm that provides input to the process of designing, developing, or delivering material aimed at influencing a recipient (either immediately or over time) is participating in the advertising process and therefore providing an advertising service. Given the diverse suite of services available to sport brands, advertising service providers range from a single person through to multinational brands. Further, as with marketing services more generally, in seeking to generate shared meaning with target audiences, it is not essential to use advertising service providers. It can all be done 'in-house' by a sport brand itself, although this has become less common, especially given the specialist demands of social media and digital advertising.

Sport brands with larger branding budgets tend to avail themselves of a bigger range of services on offer given both the costs involved and the investment needed to secure positive returns. Smaller brands will also likely pursue external advertising services, conscious that in a competitive environment, developing some form of brand awareness and positive brand image remains critical to long-term brand equity. A wide variety of advertising mediums ensures that just about every sport brand can afford some kind of advertising support. A small club or association can advertise 'online' through 'AdSense' or 'Google Ads' (online advertising services, developed by Google), while at the same time inserting messages 'offline' in a local newspaper.

Advertising services agencies and other providers do not see themselves as separate from the other branding activities their clients undertake, given they understand that the nature of communication is intertwined with brand value and media convergence. Many providers will advocate to be involved in a client's brand strategy formulation in order to add value that aligns with a longer-term ambition.

Similarly, given the relatively large number of stakeholders intertwined with sporting brands, partners can assist in advertising by using their specialist skills. For example, media broadcasters are typically expert in understanding the power of advertising, and having invested in a brand by choosing to broadcast or partner with it, are vested in its success. Media services themselves are a separate service category to assist in branding.

Media services for sport branding

Auxiliary services related to media aim to leverage the effects of branding communications by using converging brand messages through multiple (1) paid, (2) owned, and (3) earned media. Most sport brands want to maximise the effects of their branding communications by deploying several channels at once in a kind of branding equivalent to a military 'pincer' movement.

This triumvirate approach to media is a relatively new development in marketing, where once media was thought of specifically as channels of communication such as television, radio, or billboards. The beauty of the paid/owned/earned approach is that it allows a sport brand to think of their communication points in a synergistic fashion. Rather than considering the intricacy of each medium, the strategic focus turns to maximising the resources they have bought (paid media), those that they have established (owned media), and, most importantly of all, those that they have been able to seed and promulgate through their community (earned media). We explore all of these, noting that using this approach will be a critical path in the communication actions of a modern sporting brand.

Paid media is any paid-for marketing communication activity (online or offline) designed to promote a brand. For example, paid media for a campaign could include a combination of outdoor ads on public transport, radio and direct mail (offline investment) and remarketing, search engine marketing (paid search), a Facebook ad, and a pre-roll ad on YouTube or a streaming site (online investment). In all these cases, a brand is investing in a message, whether through digital or traditional means, and seeking to generate a return on that commitment. Theoretically, for every dollar invested, a dollar or more should be returned, but there are times when a brand may not recoup this investment in return for a greater outcome, such as the establishment of a new brand which requires considerable resources, or a brand battle that sees the demise of a competitor. Paid media needs to be carefully explored, as sport brands are notoriously poor at measuring their return-on-investment. This is understandable in an industry where wins and losses are usually more important than profits and losses. It stands to reason that when paying for media exposure, a sport brand must be very clear what is being communicated and how it will be communicated to enrich the brand. Expert guidance is usually helpful here, particularly in the digital field where paid media is typically sourced through a bidding process.

Owned media is any marketing communication asset owned by the brand. In the offline world, owned media could be retail stores within stadiums, carry bags for merchandise, brochures, or, even in the case of major sporting teams, their own radio and television stations. In the online world, owned media could be the brand's website, company blogs, apps that have been developed, and the curated presence on various forms of social media, such as Facebook and Instagram. Sporting brands are typically strong in terms of owned media given that the assets they possess tend to relate to marketable merchandise, highly popular fan sites, and apps that have been produced to generate engagement with fans and spectators. One of the challenges for sporting brands is that a devout fan may never actually transact monetarily with the team that they follow, choosing instead to follow from a distance as passionately as a fan who attends every match.

Owned media allows sporting brands to interact with distant fans, offering services and insights that can be monetised, such as highlights, player insights, and other appealing value propositions. Once again, expert advice is helpful to make use of these avenues. It is worth noting that a decision often needs to be made with owned media as to whether the assets should be owned by a sporting brand or conglomerated and owned by a league, or similar governing body, as a way of offering standardised content and experience. Many leagues around the world use a common template for their websites, for example, provided by a league sponsor to facilitate a simple way of generating content creation. Bigger organisations, such as Chelsea Football Club, however, tend to prefer owning their own channels, with the biggest of clubs offering 24/7 access on networks that can reach audiences around the world.

Earned media in the offline world constitutes publicity or 'buzz' generated through public relations in the form of media releases, product releases, and other appearances (usually by players and coaches / managers). In the online world, earned media also includes the ever-powerful concept of word-of-mouth (mouse), which is increasingly being stimulated through viral and social media marketing, and conversations in other online communities such as fan forums. Not surprisingly, of all the three media types, earned media is the one that marketers salivate over the most. Earned media is powerful, persuasive, and relatively low cost given the multiplier effect of a viral message being passed through a community. Like good branding itself, earned media does not happen by accident. It requires careful curation, seeding of content, and, in many cases, the willingness for a sport marketer to hand control of the brand over to the fans, giving them access to unfettered content and the encouragement to produce material that will engage and earn impressions. The NBA, as we have noted, provides the benchmark, pushing its teams and athletes to engage with social media while stimulating influencers of all sizes to take material and turn it into consumable chunks for the broader community.[8] The approach is ideal in a world where entertainment is moving online, and products like sport go well beyond traditional boundaries.

The paid, owned, and earned framework is a logical set of strategic categories that can address all existing offline and online marketing communication touchpoints, while, at the same time, caters to future touchpoints as they are developed. The framework is becoming the standard approach to how brands plan on interacting with their customers, particularly as they seek synergistic links between a wide range of media forms.

Direct marketing services for sport branding

Any marketing material sent directly to a current or potential customer (fan) designed to create an immediate response may be considered direct marketing.[9] Responses range on a continuum between a purchase decision (or progression towards some form of exchange), and some form of dismissal (e.g., ignoring the content, disposing of it, or similar). Direct marketing may therefore be seen as a subset of integrated marketing communications incorporating marketing research, segmentation, evaluation, and so on.[10] Direct marketing can use any form, or combination of channel – from print to broadcast to digital – to both transmit an offer and elicit a response.

While it may seem strange to single out direct marketing here (after all, it is essentially a form of marketing itself), it deserves unique treatment because it typically seeks an instantaneous response. Thus far, we have spoken of branding as being a process that builds up over time, carefully curated and measured, like filling a bucket with one droplet of water at a time. Direct marketing pushes much of that thinking aside and literally asks a consumer to respond 'yes' or 'no' immediately. With direct marketing you never die wondering. The concern of some critics that marketing can build value but not necessarily unlock that potential is overcome in a direct marketing scenario, presuming enough people say 'yes.'

The role of direct marketing in sport branding has transformed radically over the past decade given the growth of data, media platforms, and digital channels. As a consequence, while direct marketing services formerly occupied a niche segment within mainstream marketing, it has since moved to the forefront of branding. Many will argue that as technology grows, it will become the dominant form of marketing.

The key advantage of direct marketing (and its various channels such as direct mail, detailed next) lies with its active approach to engaging consumers. It has proven effective in moving recipients swiftly through the behavioural stages of consumption, from being alerted to a need or want, through to purchase.

There might also be some benefits in 'engaging the senses' through direct marketing. While activating multiple senses occurs through direct marketing, it does so in ways similar to other forms of contemporary communication where senses can be actively provoked. Billboards, for example, are now often interactive, samples in grocery stores remain powerfully engaging across all the senses, and modern digital technologies can bring experiences to life in interactive ways that also have the benefit of directly tracking (and responding to) consumer involvement.

Direct mail and messaging services for sport branding

Usually treated as a subset of direct marketing, direct mail uses specialised messages to target audiences based on one or several important commonalities in order to prompt a particular response. For sport marketers, direct mail messaging – both traditional and digital – is a powerful channel given the wealth of information they normally have on their databases about fans, supporters, and participants. For example, all junior members of a club might receive an offer to bring a grandparent to a match for a reduced ticket price, or members of a club might be encouraged to introduce a 'new' member and receive a gift. In general, the more targeted the appeal, the more likely it will trigger a favourable response. Nevertheless, plenty of direct mail campaigns end up discarded without a second look because they do not speak to the needs of the recipients. Direct mail can also be specifically addressed or remain unaddressed (e.g., 'to the householder'), although the former is clearly preferable given its personalisation and the range of devices and means through which such messaging can be delivered.

Direct mail messaging can seek an immediate reaction (a form of direct-response media), or it can merely try to inform, persuade, or remind, with longer-term goals in mind. It would be presumptuous to assume that all direct mail pursues an immediate response. Direct mail is not always a form of direct marketing as it can simply work as a medium that transmits advertising information. And, like all advertising, the more personalised the better. As a result, direct mail can be both a part of direct marketing when it acts as a means of seeking an immediate response, and a form of advertising service when it transmits marketing information. These boundaries are blurry as no brand would go to the trouble and expense of contacting consumers without the hope of some kind of positive response, even if just in the form of changed perceptions. While the speed and immediacy of a response may vary, the overarching goal remains to foster an exchange process to build and sustain long-term brand value.

For sporting brands, the personalised connection of direct mail messaging offers a powerful conduit, even if in other parts of the business world its scope is being rethought. Coaches, players, presidents, and other senior figures in sporting organisations realise the importance of staying connected to their fan base and often use direct mail messaging as a way of reinforcing branding intentions. For season-ticket holders, the receipt of material that facilitates that relationship – a card, lanyard, scarf, sticker, or other tangible element – is normally still dispatched by post and highly anticipated. The same can be said for a message from a sporting club that appears on a mobile smart device, or is directed towards an individual on a social media account where fans congregate, bringing an element of personalisation to branding. In an increasingly impersonal world, direct mail messaging stands as a personal touch that should be exploited by sports to reinforce their brand as offering a genuine two-way relationship of shared value.

Sport branding and digital channels

Following the current trend of radical upshifts in technology, digital branding will continue to grow exponentially. In fact, given the vast quantity of consumer information collected from digital browsing and transactions, as well as records of physical purchases, it is certain that digital channels will proliferate. Nevertheless, the principles and techniques outlined in this book hold the same currency, albeit directed through alternative media.

Digital sport branding involves the use of electronic media technologies, tools, and channels in branding activities. However, successful digital branding utilises the same principles as those using analogue channels. Great branding has to do more than just use new technology. Like all branding, it has to respond to the needs and expectations of sport consumers. Just adding another channel to the branding messages being pumped out to sport consumers will do nothing more than add to the noise. Digital channels are therefore best employed where they can take advantage of the new ways that consumers want and expect to engage with various kinds of information, consumption avenues, and entertainment content. For example, sport consumers also tend to want personalised experiences, interactivity, choice and control, the opportunity to multitask, and to gain access to user-generated content.

The critical point to remember is that like all other forms of analogue branding, consumers just tune out mass communications and untargeted sales pitches. It does not really matter whether they appear as a pop-up ad, arrive through social media, emblazon shop windows, or throw shade over the freeway. The presence of new technological tools should therefore sharpen the way branding managers think about the pace of marketing and the nature of interaction and communication with consumers.

A plethora of new hardware and software technologies along with advances in information networks and broadcasting will magnify the options for sport branding initiatives. Many of them will close the gap between product and fan, allowing viewers to not only soak up personalised sporting experiences taking place anywhere in the world, but also receive bespoke branding messages along with it. Creative branding and product placement will no doubt continue to rise. Where once athletes stopped the clock to painstakingly retie an apparently soundly fastened shoelace in order to acquire some camera time for their sponsored brand, shortly fans will be exposed to branded footage from state-of-the-art cameras embedded in the contact lenses of participating athletes.

Some new technologies and digital channels will offer advantages for sport branding, but there will also remain dangers associated with clumsy and cavalier use. Sport organisations must have the fundamental branding tools – an integrated communications strategy – to ensure that the associations they deliver to fans reflect desired needs and attractive benefits.

Conclusion – from co-creation to strategy

In this final chapter we noted that the future of branding has arrived through value co-creation based on the engagement between consumers and brands. Sport brands are particularly well placed to take advantage of this paradigmatic shift given that they understand the need to co-opt consumers into creating favourable, unique, and strong associations. If one was to spend a long time thinking about sports, it is apparent that many are patently absurd, from grown adults striking a small ball with a range of metal sticks towards a small hole on a manicured piece of grass, through to attempts to keep an inflated ball off the sand at the beach. Sport, its equipment, its ancillary products, and many of the experiences it offers are appealing not because of their direct offering, but for what they stand for in terms of achievement, perfection, aspiration, enjoyment, camaraderie, and, as we discussed, a positive form of stress.

The future of branding will be best exploited by sport brands, who stand as entertainment titans in a highly competitive industry. Like all branding though, the question that will be asked as co-creation delivers a new form of value is who actually owns a brand beyond its legal status. The willingness to release a brand to the custody of its customers is a dramatic shift, but one which can result in branding that exceeds traditional elements, moving it from tangible transactions to innate and intangible relationships that form bonds that are difficult to break and immensely valuable to a variety of stakeholders eager to share in the magic. Even the most hardened of business executive or wizened shopper can feel a shiver of excitement and electricity when entering Manchester United's 'Theatre of Dreams,' driving down 'Magnolia Lane' at Augusta National Golf Club, or seeing the New Zealand All Blacks perform their Haka before a rugby match. Sport has the passion to ignite branding in ways that no product can surpass, and the pathway ahead is littered with opportunity.

In helping to navigate the tricky path of communication that exists in the contemporary world, we explained that advertising is an important part of marketing that deals with purposeful communication to selected audiences. Advertising also sits within a mix of elements that make up 'integrated marketing communications,' the purpose being to ensure that in a competitive environment, the offerings of a brand resonate substantively and synergistically with its customers. An increased complexity in branding has led to more options in how the marketing communications mix is executed, with greater emphasis now on ensuring consumers are targeted through a range of interrelated channels. Sport enterprises of all sizes and types are clients of marketing and advertising services. The firms that offer marketing services are expanding, or, at least, reshaping their offerings to ensure that the focus is on client outcomes that match the new opportunities, rather than just providing traditional functional processes.

We further highlighted that direct marketing, as its name suggests, is a component of branding that plays a significant role given its capacity to rapidly engage consumers towards action. Direct marketing's role has transformed in the past decade, given the growth of data, media platforms, and a clearer understanding by brands as to how marketing planning must be fully integrated. Direct mail is a subset of direct marketing as a form of direct-response media, and can act more broadly to simply distribute advertising material. Direct mail's reach can be precise or broad, dependent upon the circumstances, and it can also seek immediate action or simply deliver more passive information, again dependent upon the strategic considerations in place.

Providers of advertising and marketing services have adapted to a new environment by guiding their clients through the numerous purchasing options, communication platforms, and offers being faced by consumers. Direct marketing and direct mail providers are thus expansionary in their view of what must be provided, blending services and consultative processes to ensure currency and a place in what are commonly called 'multi-channel campaigns' – communication methods that seek to synergistically blend mediums in order to capture audiences in a variety of ways.

Strong brands, especially those with a digitised presence, have an advantage in wielding emerging digital media. They are well placed to transfer the goodwill, or brand equity, that they have established across to new access points. This process is akin to traditional 'bricks and mortar' retailers (established retailers with a shopfront presence) who have successfully transferred their brands online, taking with them the hard won, established brand associations (such as authority, reliability, and trust) that have come to be valued by their customers.

Final comments

A brand arrives in a symbolic package including a name, supplementary descriptive words, a logo, and other designs and styling that differentiate it from other products and suppliers. Its purpose is to provide a signal and an anchor: a signal to customers, fans, and potential consumers to attract their attention and condition it against a set of desirable brand associations; an anchor in that the brand assumes a definitive place in consumers' minds and elicits a predictable response whenever they encounter it. Ideally, the encounter invokes all the associations that a brand has worked hard to convey.

In short, a successful and powerful sport brand stands for something to fans and consumers; it has meaning. Of course, meaning can be tremendously powerful, and when it hits the mark, it can yield sustainable value over time through the loyalty of those who repeat purchase. Brand specialists in marketing view such value as brand equity. While difficult to pin down and hard to measure, brand equity means that a brand has become more than the sum of its products and their immediate sales. Brand equity is the strategic equivalent of owning an asset more valuable than most physical investments could be. Establishing an objective measure of brand equity remains challenging, but typically involves a concoction of factors including brand awareness, perceived quality of the products, brand associations, and brand loyalty, sometimes complemented with market behaviour measures like market share.

As we have outlined in this book, the process of cultivating a sport brand and managing its presence is known as branding. Another way of looking at it is to think of branding as the process of managing the relationship between a sport enterprise and its consumers. Branding occupies the territory where products and services connect with those who use them, and, critically, those who might use them. When the relationship works, we might say that the sport enterprise enjoys a degree of brand loyalty, which means that their brand's products have accumulated some resilience, and consumers of them are likely to maintain their purchasing even through change and the arrival of alternatives. In the sport world, we call these consumers 'fans.'

Brand loyalty represents an attempt to measure the level of attachment that a consumer has to a brand and its products. As noted earlier, it also serves as a proxy for the likelihood that a consumer might switch to another brand if given an incentive to do so. In addition to the ongoing benefits that come with a set of loyal consumers whose consistent purchasing behaviour can be relied upon, brand loyalty also saves on branding and other marketing costs. Keeping loyal customers or fans is cheaper than creating them in the first place. Conversely, it is highly expensive for competing brands to change the allegiances of loyal fans.

Perhaps more than many other products and services, sport has a natural affinity with branding because it stimulates a higher level of brand loyalty. In sport, perceived brand performance, personal identification, and familial histories contribute to stronger attitudes towards a brand, which more easily leads to repeat purchasing and loyalty. Where sport brands deliver a physical contest, the product is consumed (usually) live on site or through a media channel. Other sport enterprises represent brands that provide products or other related services, from equipment and apparel to entertainment and gaming. Sometimes the products rely on the unpredictable character of the sporting contest, while others are expected to maintain strict levels of unwavering quality. Irrespective of the sport product's nature, and the kind of associations it strives to convey, the branding process remains the same. It is also noteworthy that sport brands can be sufficiently influential to command sponsorship from non-sporting entities who desire to link their own brand associations to those of the sporting product. Some of the sporting brand's associations can rub off on the sponsor's brand. As a result, branding can work through sport as well as within it.

Amidst all the marketing terminology we have highlighted, two important concepts that are instructive in understanding how sport branding works are brand image and brand identity. Brand image reflects how a brand is perceived by prospective and existing consumers. Brand identity specifies that perception. The former is what occupies a consumer's mind when they notice or think about a brand. The latter is what the brand tries to communicate as deployed through their products and benefits, through the custodian sporting enterprise, through symbols, and through personal inferences of the kind that would be applied to a person rather than an intangible brand. The collection works to create a metaphorical 'personality' for a brand that has life and agency of its own. Human nature ensures that consumers feel greater affinity to a brand when its identity resonates at a personal level. When consumers can recognise a brand, they might be described as brand aware. Brand awareness can range from a consumer's ability to recognise or identify a brand without prompting, to their ability to link a brand to a specific identity. Other measures provide some further nuances such as recall, 'top of mind' recognition, perceptions of brand dominance, brand familiarity, and brand knowledge.

A critical part of the branding process has to do with the associations that become linked to a brand. Associations appear in the minds of consumers when they encounter a brand; they form the constituents and contents of a brand's identity, albeit channelled through consumers' perceptions of the brand image. Associations can range in nature, but typically include a character, personality, consumer segment, feeling, product characteristic and benefit, or symbol.

Branding plays a decisive role in the sport marketplace by assisting consumers to identify products and to form favourable associations towards them. It helps sport enterprises build positive and valuable brand features, such as authority, status, quality, trust, and reliability. Sport enterprises can further use successful brand elements to introduce new products. For example, 'device marks' – the symbolic (mostly) visual representations of brand – are linked to the product itself and can serve multiple, interrelated roles. Notably, they help identify the brand, represent the image and associated quality of the brand to customers, decorate the product to make it visually appealing, provide a launching pad for future endeavours, and, ultimately, as a result of the foregoing, enhance the brand equity of sport enterprises capable of creating positive associations with the brand elements.

Sport brands are the symbolic correlates of sport enterprises. They represent what any given sport or sport organisation means to someone who thinks about them. In this respect, sport brands reside at the intersection of consumers' thoughts and market forces – an intangible but powerful transformation from the individual content of minds to collective commercial value. A sport brand is therefore the fulcrum upon which the lever of fandom is balanced. By extension, a sport's brand is its lifeblood, the beating heart of its health. Although difficult to execute, there is no more important task than branding sport for its custodians.

Notes

1   Vargo, S., & Lusch, R. (2004). Evolving to a new dominant logic. *Journal of Marketing, 68*, 1–17.
2   Smith, A.C.T., Stavros, C., & Westberg, K. (2017). *Brand Fans*. Cham: Springer.
3   Ritzer, G., & Jurgenson, N. (2010). Production, consumption, prosumption: The nature of capitalism in the age of the digital 'prosumer.' *Journal of Consumer Culture, 10*(1), 13–26.
4   Retrieved from https://www.wilson.com/en-us/explore/golf/driver-vs-driver.
5   Anzilotti, E. (2016). *How the NBA's progressivism is helping it thrive*. Retrieved from https://www.theatlantic.com/business/archive/2016/06/nba-progressivism/487610/.
6   Smith, A.C.T., Stavros, C., & Westberg, K. (2017). *Brand Fans*. Cham: Springer.
7   Pritchard, M.P., & Stinson, J.L. (Eds.). (2013). *Leveraging Brands in Sport Business*. London: Routledge.
8   Maese, R. (2018). *NBA Twitter: A sports bar that doesn't close, where the stars pull up a seat next to you*. Retrieved from https://www.washingtonpost.com/news/sports/wp/2018/05/31/nba-twitter-a-sports-bar-that-doesnt-close-where-the-stars-pull-up-a-seat-next-to-you/?utm_term=.4e2b-f238ac5b.
9   Chitty, B, Luck, E., Barker, N., Valos, M., & Shimp T.A. (2015). *Integrated Marketing Communications*. Melbourne, VIC: Cengage.
10 Belch, G.E., Belch, M.A., Kerr, G., & Powell, I. (2009). *Advertising and Promotion*. Sydney, NSW: McGraw Hill.

Index

Printed in the United States
by Baker & Taylor Publisher Services